A SUKKAH IN THE SHADOW OF SAINT IGNATIUS

Essays on the History of Jewish-Christian Relations

A joint publication of The Joan and Ralph Lane Center for Catholic Social Thought and the Ignatian Tradition & The Swig Program in Jewish Studies and Social Justice

Edited by
Jeremy P. Brown

Published by the
UNIVERSITY OF SAN FRANCISCO PRESS
Joan and Ralph Lane Center
for Catholic Social Thought and the Ignatian Tradition
&
Swig Program in Jewish Studies and Social Justice

University of San Francisco
2130 Fulton Street
San Francisco, CA 94117-1080
www.usfca.edu/lane-center

Collection copyright © 2020
ISBN 978-1-949643-51-0 | paperback
ISBN 978-1-949643-52-7 | epub

Authors retain the copyright to their individual essays.

Published by the University of San Francisco Press through the Joan and Ralph Lane Center for Catholic Social Thought and the Ignatian Tradition of the University of San Francisco.

The Lane Center Series promotes the center's mission to advance the scholarship and application of the Catholic intellectual tradition in the church and society with an emphasis on social concerns. The series features essays by Lane Center scholars, guest speakers, and USF faculty. It serves as a written archive of Lane Center events and programs and allows the work of the center to reach a broader audience.

Cover: Photography by Arvin Temkar.

The Lane Center Series

Published by the Joan and Ralph Lane Center for Catholic Social Thought and the Ignatian Tradition at the University of San Francisco, the Lane Center Series explores intersections of faith and social justice. Featuring essays that bridge interdisciplinary research and community engagement, the series serves as a resource for social analysis, theological reflection, and education in the Jesuit tradition.

Visit the Lane Center's website to download each volume and view related resources at www.usfca.edu/lane-center

Volumes

Beyond Borders:
Reflections on the Resistance & Resilience Among Immigrant Youth and Families

Catholic Identity in Context:
Vision and Formation for the Common Good

Today I Gave Myself Permission to Dream:
Race and Incarceration in America

Islam at Jesuit Colleges and Universities

Pope Francis and the Future of Catholicism in the United States:
The Challenge of Becoming a Church for the Poor

The Declaration on Christian Education: Reflections by the Institute for Catholic Education Leadership and the Joan and Ralph Lane Center for Catholic Studies and Social Thought

Dorothy Day:
A Life and Legacy

Editor

Erin Brigham
Lane Center, University of San Francisco

Editorial Board

KIMBERLY RAE CONNOR
School of Management, University of San Francisco

THERESA LADRIGAN-WHELPLEY
Salve Regina University

CATHERINE PUNSALAN-MANLIMOS
University of Detroit Mercy

LISA FULLAM
Jesuit School of Theology of Santa Clara University

DONAL GODFREY, S.J.
University Ministry, University of San Francisco

MARK MILLER
Department of Theology and Religious Studies,
University of San Francisco

MARK POTTER
Newton Country Day School of the Sacred Heart, Newton MA

FRANK TURNER, S.J.
Delegate for the Jesuit Intellectual Apostolate, London

Table of Contents

Acknowledgements 1

Letters between the directors of the
Lane Center and Swig Program 3
ERIN BRIGHAM AND AARON HAHN TAPPER

Infancy Stories of Jesus: Apocrypha
and Toledot Yeshu in Medieval Europe 15
NATALIE E. LATTERI

Beyond the Pale: Hasidism, Neo-Hasidism
and Jewish-Christian Dialogue 53
ARIEL EVAN MAYSE

Jewish Historical Testimony at the Table
of Christian Hospitality 91
JEREMY P. BROWN

Acknowledgements

I am grateful to the Swig Program in Jewish Studies and Social Justice, the Joan and Ralph Lane Center for Catholic Social Thought and the Ignatian Tradition, the USF Department of Theology and Religious Studies, and especially the Jesuit Foundation for their generous backing of both the Speaker Series in the History of Jewish-Christian Relations, and the present volume. I acknowledge too the support of the USF History Department, and from the broader San Francisco community, Lehrhaus Judaica, Grace Cathedral, Congregation Beth Shalom, and San Francisco Interfaith Council.

The scholars who brought their research and insights for the 2017 series were Eva Mrocek (UC Davis), Deena Aranoff (Graduate Theological Union), and Naomi Seidman (then Graduate Theological Union, now University of Toronto). 2018 scholars were Roberto Mata (University of Santa Clara), Natalie Latteri (then University of New Mexico, now USF), and Ariel Evan Mayse (Stanford University). I am particularly grateful to Latteri and Mayse for developing their talks into essays for this publication. Members of the USF faculty who participated as respondents included Aysha Hidayatullah, Katrina Olds, Erin Brigham, and Paolo Gamberini.

Two individuals were instrumental in bringing the series to fruition and seeing this volume to publication: Aaron Hahn Tapper and Erin Brigham. I have learned a great deal over the past three years from our work together, both personally and professionally. Both Hahn Tapper and Brigham made themselves available to the project without limits, always with tremendous grace, understanding, and humor. Their feedback at every stage contributed in substantial ways to a fine set of results. Though we set out from a place of mutual respect, my esteem for these scholars has only grown through our collaboration.

Oren Kroll-Zeldin provided sound advice and critical support on several occasions.

Lastly, I am indebted to the administrative efficiency and kindness of Monica Doblado and Alison Cunningham.

—Jeremy P. Brown, Frankfurt, Germany
24th of Tevet, 5780; January 22, 2020

Letters between Erin Brigham,* the director of Lane Center, and Aaron Hahn Tapper,** the director of the Swig Program

Dear Erin,

 I appreciate our having this opportunity to converse about this intriguing collection of essays, which emerged out of our spring 2017 and spring 2018 University of San Francisco Speaker Series in the History of Jewish-Christian Relations. As you know, each of these two spring semesters we offered a three-part series where scholars addressed the phenomenon of inter-communal relations between Jews and Christians in the ancient, medieval, and modern periods, an academic program dedicated to promoting a historical-critical ethos for studying and teaching Jewish-Christian relations writ large. Offered through USF's Swig Program in Jewish Studies and Social Justice, which I direct, these six lectures were co-sponsored by the Joan and Ralph Lane Center for Catholic Social Thought and the Ignatian Tradition (which you direct), as well as the Jesuit Foundation and the Department of Theology & Religious Studies. For me, the topics addressed under the umbrella of the ancient and medieval periods

---

*   Erin Brigham, PhD is Executive Director of the Joan and Ralph Lane Center for Catholic Social Thought and the Ignatian Tradition at the University of San Francisco. She is also Chief Mission Officer of USF. She has taught Catholic theology and social thought since 2008.

** Aaron Hahn Tapper is the Mae and Benjamin Swig Professor in Jewish Studies and the founding Director of the Swig Program in Jewish Studies and Social Justice at USF. An educator for more than two decades, his primary academic interest is the intersection between identity formation, social justice, and marginalized groups.

directly connect to the contemporary period, that is Jewish-Christian Relations in twenty-first-century America.

Although this series was conceived, shaped, and implemented almost single-handedly by teacher and scholar par excellence, Swig JSSJ Program faculty member Professor Jeremy P. Brown—who is also the editor of this book—it was incredibly important to me that the Lane Center, under your leadership, didn't blink when approached to come on board as our chief co-sponsor. Throughout my thirteen years on our Jesuit Catholic university campus I have come to take such support for granted. As such, I'd like to express my gratitude to you, the Lane Center, and our larger campus community for consistently supporting Jewish Studies at USF. Along these lines, it is important to note that, founded in 1977, our Jewish Studies program was the first program and endowed chair in Jewish Studies established at a Catholic-identified college or university campus worldwide. (In 2008, when we were re-established as the Swig Program in Jewish Studies and Social Justice, we again broke historical ground, this time becoming the first academic program in the world to formally link Jewish Studies with Social Justice). It's as if expect this amazing support, one of my notable blindspots. For this I apologize.

I offer this *mea culpa* first and foremost because it is important to lay it out there. Second, I submit this admission because I want what I am about to say to be understood within the context of my appreciation. In other words, although I am about to offer some personal reflections on Jewish-Christian relations using an analytical lens bordering on the critical, I do so with the knowledge that I am able to do this precisely because of the safe space I have experienced as a Jew who directs a Jewish Studies program at a Jesuit Catholic university (located in a Christian-majority country). And I do so with a deep and sincere recognition of my time at USF since 2007, which has been incredible, and an understanding that everything I am able to do at USF with Jewish Studies is due to the support of the USF administration and larger community.

It must also be said that I fully recognize that I come to this project with emotional baggage rooted in the violent historical backdrop of interactions between Jews and Christians for millennia, contact that has notably ended in death for Jews at the hands of Christians far too many times. (I am also cognizant of the textual evidence of Jews dismissing Christians, found, among other places, in Natalie Latteri's, "Infancy Stories of Jesus: Apocrypha and the *Toledot Yeshu* in Medieval Europe" and Ariel Mayse's "Beyond the Pale: Hasidism, Neo-Hasidism and Jewish-Christian Dialogue," both of which are also found in this volume).

This all said... As an educator who focuses his course work and research on contemporary issues, perhaps it should not be surprising that of the three essays in this collection Jeremy Brown's "Jewish Historical Testimony at the Table of Christian Hospitality" deeply resonates with me, particularly his thesis question related to the "hospitality complex that binds the differentiated domain of Jewish historical testimony in research and teaching about religion conducted at Christian institutions," as well as such statements as "there are serious risks at stake when the academic discipline of Jewish Studies yokes itself to performing the 'guest labor' of Christian conscience."

Brown begins his essay with an epigraph written by Aristotle, "The guest will judge better of a feast than the cook." This idea reflects a core aspect of my experiences at USF. To take it one step further, the vantage point of a member of a minority community in a given space is far different, on the whole, than that of a member of a majority community. Although the guest/host dyad is different than the minority/majority one, and sometimes these two pairings are distinct, for me they are one and the same in this particular situation; being a member of the Jewish community on a Catholic-identified campus lends itself to particular perceptions that I would not have, say, if I was a member of the campus community at Yeshiva University, for example, a Jewish-majority learning environment located in New York City (an urban center with the second most Jews of any city worldwide, and most in the US). Put another way, to some degree I have experienced my time at USF as a "guest" at a "host" institution.[1]

In this regard, my experiences at USF have been shaped by countless on-campus micro-events. This has included those linked to seemingly mundane scheduling issues, such as the recent scheduling of the December 2019 USF graduation ceremony to take place on a Friday evening, which, for me, corresponds to the Jewish Sabbath (*Shabbat*), a time I spend with my family. This has also included theologically weighted rituals, such as choosing the following verse to open the August 2019 USF Mass of the Holy Spirit—especially when taking into account that this university- and community-wide event included the participation of our new campus Rabbi-in-Residence for the first time, and she was given a prominent place on the church pulpit alongside our university's President—"There is neither Jew nor Gentile, neither slave nor free, nor is there male and female, for you are all one in Christ Jesus" (Gal. 3:28). As a scholar committed to the idea that there are multiple ways to interpret events and texts, I know that this approach can apply to these specific contexts as well; I know that one can interpret this verse, and the choice to include it in this ritual, in a deeply positive manner. In other words, my own personal negative experience in regard to both is not conclusive. And yet, for me, as a Jew directing a Jewish Studies program at a Catholic-identified school, these two occurrences—two of thousands I've witnessed since I came to campus—are reflective of a basic systemic orientation toward Jews as "guests" on campus, even if not intended as such.

I am going to stop here for now. Looking forward to hearing where this meets you, Erin.

In peace,
Aaron

---

[1] On a different but related point, I am also quite aware of my multiple privileges vis-à-vis social identities that are not explicitly linked to my Jewish identity, in terms of gender, etc.

Dear Aaron,

Thank you for initiating a dialogue on this compelling volume of essays. It was an honor to co-sponsor the University of San Francisco Speaker Series on the History of Jewish-Christian relations in collaboration with the Swig Program in Jewish Studies and Social Justice and our colleagues in the Department of Theology and Religious Studies. I recognize it as a concrete expression of the Lane Center's commitment to fostering critical engagement with faith, social justice, and the Jesuit mission of the University.

Under your leadership, the Swig Program in Jewish Studies and Social Justice has been a leader in advancing the University's engagement with human rights, equity, and empowerment of marginalized communities. These values resonate deeply with those espoused and developed in modern Catholic social thought. In my work with the Lane Center, I have found that engaging faith and social justice has been a primary point of entry for people to encounter the Jesuit Catholic mission of the university. The social teaching of Catholicism, rooted in a fundamental commitment to inclusive human flourishing, holds out the promise of an alternative to expressions of religion that have been disempowering, discriminatory, and violent. As a theologian in the Catholic tradition, I am compelled to ask myself: if we are not looking honestly and critically at these expressions of our tradition, are we doing our job as a Catholic university? The History of Jewish-Christian Relations Speaker Series created a context for this encounter, reflection, and analysis.

One of the initial goals of the series, articulated by Dr. Jeremy Brown, was "to prompt critical conversations about the tensions which exist between, on the one hand, the promotion of an historically *uncritical* sense of religious identity and, on the other hand, the pursuit of social justice values." Continuing this effort, his essay in this volume challenges me to reflect on whether my own theological commitment to translating the content of Catholicism into an inclusive and meaningful encounter for a secular, socially-engaged, and religiously diverse audience creates enough space for critical assessment. We both know that the history of Jewish-Christian relations shapes the present, disallowing the assumption of social harmony even within Christian-influenced spaces that embrace a theology of religious pluralism and prioritize human rights as the basis for justice.

The micro-events you named that reinforce your experience as a "guest" at a Catholic university challenge us all to take seriously the task of promoting inclusion and equity across all identities as an expression of the University's mission. I recall an event we co-sponsored with the Cultural Centers on the theme of Christian dominance. The facilitator welcomed students into the room as Christmas music played in the background—something that generally seems subtle to some of us became recognizably exclusive and distracting to most of us involved in the activity. Students were eager to discuss cultural expressions of Christian dominance, including those couched within the framework of religious liberty. The incongruence with USF's Jesuit Catholic commitment to social justice was not lost on them.

Brown insists that we move beyond a conciliatory approach to Jewish-Christian relations and effectively demonstrates inadequate frameworks for interreligious reconciliation. Yet, I am compelled to take seriously the challenge Arturo Sosa, SJ, issued to all Jesuit universities: to be sources of reconciliation as an expression of their mission.[2] Some might argue that the work of historical analysis is central to the task of reconciliation, but that any conciliatory consequence of a speaker series like ours should be considered a secondary outcome of a primary emphasis on historical truth. I am wondering how helpful it is to parse out primary and secondary aims in such a context, given the interdependence of knowledge and action, truth and reconciliation. I don't know if my questioning flows from my identity as a theologian rather than a historian or if it comes from the privileged place I occupy as a self-identified Catholic in a Catholic university.

I look forward to continuing this conversation with you, Aaron.

Sincerely,

Erin

---

[2] Arturo Sosa, SJ, "The University as a Source of a Reconciled life," Address to the World Meeting of Universities Entrusted to the Society of Jesus in Loyola (July 10, 2018).

Dear Erin,

I appreciate your voicing many things here, not the least of which is your commitment to critical self-assessment from your vantage point as a scholar of Catholicism, and a self-identified Catholic, at a Catholic university. I am equally comforted by your voicing a goal that we share in common: to work toward making our campus—and, of course, the world—a place where communities experience inclusivity, social-engagement, and meaning.

When I pivot toward my more dominant social identities (i.e., white, male, cisgender, heterosexual, etc.) I feel we are on relatively equal footing in the context of this specific discussion of my feeling as if I am a "guest" on campus. When I engage the question of critical self-assessment from my Ashkenazi Jewish social identity, participating in a similar project of reflexivity but as a Jew at a Catholic university, I feel that self-reflection and self-criticism—especially of my own Jewish communities—has the potential to take on a different tone. At the same time, I consider myself an educator, perhaps above all else, and so whenever I step foot on our campus I feel that self-criticism (whether of myself or my Jewish community generally) is "my calling," if you will; it is something I must practice over and over again. That is to say, being self-critical of Catholicism from an individual Catholic perspective in a Catholic setting in a Christian country is different than being self-critical of Judaism from an individual Jewish perspective in a Catholic setting in a Christian country. For me, this might be the crux of why my experience at USF continues to be one of a "guest" and not a "host."

As for your introducing Arturo Sosa, SJ, into our conversation, more specifically the challenge he issues to all Jesuit universities to be sources of reconciliation as an expression of their mission, in terms of our current conversation I equally approach this from my vantage point as a Jew on a Catholic campus. Meaning, even though I am committed to interreligious reconciliation just as you are, in terms of our positionality—as a Jew and a Catholic— it is from different places, especially when talking about our work at USF. The view that any conciliatory consequence of a speaker series like ours should be considered a secondary outcome—with there needing to be a primary emphasis on historical truth—resonates with my vantage point as a Jew.

In regard to the important question of parsing out primary and secondary goals, I wonder if it is possible to genuinely get to the secondary goal (reconciliation) without first approaching the primary goal (laying one's cards on the table in terms of "historical truth"). Similarly, my understanding is that when, for example, in a given context, a Truth and Reconciliation Commission (TRC) is established, the goals are to first put truth out there—first confront the crimes, the misdeeds, the atrocities. Only then can there be tangible and sustainable reconciliation. Indeed, in those situations where TRCs are not successful in creating spaces for the historical underbelly of a country to be revealed, acknowledged, and discussed, reconciliation is nothing more than a word. I think this phenomenon can apply to Jewish-Christian relations as well. Whether the primary and secondary goals happen sequentially or simultaneously, I think both must take place for there to be sincere movement toward reconciliation.

In peace,
Aaron

Dear Aaron,

I appreciate your reflection, particularly the way in which you articulate your calling as an educator—to model the critical self-reflexivity we expect from our students. I resonate with this as a Catholic theologian and feminist—two identities that are not seamlessly reconcilable but that I am able to hold in a creative tension at USF. One of the reasons I feel at home at USF is that it allows me to explore these tensions in my research and teaching. I appreciate the freedom to engage critically and creatively the Catholic social and theological traditions in light of diverse experiences. But I keep reflecting on what you have identified as the crux of your experience as a guest at USF, in a Catholic setting, in a Christian country. It is an important reminder of the privilege of being self-critical in a space where one's identity is dominant. I think of this when I teach theories of justice and challenge my students to encounter oppressive structures—knowing that our students have diverse experiences of these realities.

I wholeheartedly agree with your point about truth as a precondition for reconciliation. My emphasis on the interconnectedness of knowledge and action was only to suggest that the process of truth-telling was itself a conciliatory act. Perhaps, this glosses over the critical value of historical honesty for its own sake, which Brown emphasizes and you rightly affirm. I agree that reconciliation can too easily become cheapened when it lacks substantive and prolonged engagement in truth-telling.

I am reminded of an article by Bryan Massingale, a leading voice for racial justice in the Catholic Church. Writing as a professor of theology at Fordham University, Massingale claims that Jesuit campuses should be "sanctuaries of truth."[3] To your point, he argues that effective reconciliation is only possible when we commit ourselves to an honest encounter with reality. This requires overcoming willful

---

[3] Bryan Massingale, "The Ignatian Witness to Truth in a Climate of Injustice" in *Conversations on Jesuit Higher Education* (August 12, 2017).

ignorance as well as implicit bias and being willing to face discomfort and conflict.

Our conversation has made me contemplate more deeply Massingale's use of the word "sanctuary"—a word that can also be cheapened by paternalistic notions of hospitality. What would it mean to be a sanctuary for truth in this context? My understanding of sanctuary is that it isn't just about sharing space but creating an alternative space together that involves mutual risk and trust. Does this create a way to move beyond hospitality? Or am I getting lost in semantics?

In gratitude,
Erin

Dear Erin,

As you correctly said to me in private, this conversation could go on indefinitely. Though I don't have a conclusion to this exchange, even a momentary one, I am left with similar thoughts and feelings to those that I had from the outset: I am grateful for having the space on this page and on campus to be myself—a Jew on a Jesuit Catholic campus—while simultaneously I am mindful of the centuries-old patterns of oppression between Jews and Catholics, actions, almost entirely, of the latter toward the former. Given our university's commitment to social justice, I feel that this mixture of feelings is both warranted and encouraged.

I am reminded of a private dinner I attended in my position as the Director of our Jewish Studies program, when a prominent member of USF—who himself is Catholic—shared his feeling that the historical experiences of Catholics in the United States are similar to those of Jews. Most of the 25 or so people in the room were Jews. I remember thinking that the speaker's intentions were surely positive. Yet his words missed the mark for me. Putting aside the deep problematics of my taking a position rooted in a hierarchy of oppression—as if his words were fallible merely because *my* people have suffered more than *his* people in terms of American history, a perspective that is challenging for countless reasons—I was struck by his lack of understanding of the fact that he said these things as a Catholic and Christian who lives in a Christian-majority country. One of my takeaways that evening was that he *didn't get it*. I understood that he was trying to connect with the Jews in the room—as if he was saying, "Hey, my people also were 'strangers in a strange land'"—but what he actually seemed to be saying to me was that he didn't understand his place of privilege, in the twenty-first-century, as a Catholic American.

I apologize for not appealing to the better nature of my angels here and leaving us in a more upbeat place. But at the same time I think that history is messy, unclear, and not necessarily peaceful. May our campus move toward greater progress for all—greater reconciliation for all communities—may we have more speaker series aimed at healing the divide between Jews and Christians, promoting truth and historicity alongside reconciliation, and may I have more partners in education and activism like you.

   Thank you, Erin.

   In peace,

   Aaron

Infancy Stories of Jesus:
Apocrypha and Toledot Yeshu in Medieval Europe

NATALIE E. LATTERI[*]

Stories of Jesus have circulated among Christians since the first century of the Common Era. Such lore functioned to provide early Christians who were eager to learn about their savior with information about his conception, life, death, and resurrection. Some made it into the canonical New Testament Gospel accounts but much of it, for one reason or another, did not. Even so, versions of many of the stories remained popular among Christians throughout the centuries and continued to supplement the biblical text while addressing the concerns of story tellers and their audience. For purposes of this paper, the entirety of these extra-canonical Christian texts is referred to simply as apocrypha. Like the canonical Gospel accounts and later hagiography, or (semi) fictional accounts of saints' lives, apocryphal stories of Jesus also offered entertainment and a type of model behavior for readers and listeners to emulate.[1]

---

[*] Natalie E. Latteri earned her PhD in History from the University of New Mexico. She teaches Jewish-Christian Relations at the University of San Francisco in the Swig Program in Jewish Studies and Social Justice. Latteri is a Fellow of the Russell J. and Dorothy S. Bilinski Foundation (2016-17) and the American Academy for Jewish Research (2015), among others.

[1] See David R. Cartlidge and J. Keith Elliott, *Art and the Christian Apocrypha* (London: Routledge, 2001), 23; Bart D. Ehrman, *Lost Scriptures: Books*

Jews from the first centuries of the Common Era on told their own, often quite similar, stories of Jesus. A loosely configured collection of such stories would come to be known as *Toledot Yeshu* (the life story of Jesus).² Scholars commonly refer to the *Toledot Yeshu* accounts as "counter narratives," or "counter gospels,"³ because they parody Christian biographies of Jesus and most likely served as the main source of information Jews had about Christian origin stories.⁴ The earliest extant accounts focus on Jesus' education and adult life. Historically these were told from a perspective of disbelief for an audience who was intent on mocking the Christian doctrine that Jesus was the prophesied Messiah of Israel.⁵ Instead of providing a template for praiseworthy thought, speech, or action in a manner that

---

    that Did Not Make It into the New Testament (Oxford: Oxford University Press, 2003), 57.

2   There has been much scholarship regarding the appropriateness of labeling late antique practitioners of Israelite religion as "Jews" before the development of Rabbinic Judaism and the codification of the talmudic texts. See, for example, Daniel Boyarin's discussions in *Dying for God: Martyrdom and the Making of Christianity and Judaism* (Stanford: Stanford University Press, 1999); and idem, *Border Lines: The Partition of Judaeo-Christianity* (Philadelphia: University of Pennsylvania Press, 2004). For the purposes of this paper, I use the term "Jew/s" to refer to any practitioner/s of Israelite religion in antiquity, later practitioners of Rabbinic Judaism, and various other Jewish sects.

3   Though David Biale coined the term, he does not believe that "counter-history" should be applied to *Toledot Yeshu* because all of the episodes therein do not have a one-to-one polemical correlation with the Gospel accounts. See, David Biale, "Counter-History and Jewish Polemics against Christianity: The *Sefer Toldot Yeshu* and the *Sefer Zerubavel*." *Jewish Social Studies* 6, no. 1 (1999): 130-45. This assessment is artificially limiting because it does not consider how the *Toledot Yeshu* might correlate with apocryphal stories of Jesus.

4   See Jonatan M. Benarroch, "God and His Son: Christian Affinities in the Shaping of the Sava and Yanuka Figures in the Zohar," *Jewish Quarterly Review* 107, no. 1 (2017): 39, 57.

5   Michael Meerson and Peter Schäfer, introduction to *Toledot Yeshu: The Life Story of Jesus*, vol. 1, ed. Michael Meerson and Peter Schäfer (Tübingen: Mohr Siebeck, 2014), 47.

resembled the apocrypha, *Toledot Yeshu* served as cautionary tales—models of what not to do should another messianic pretender arise. Despite these functional differences, episodic similarities in the stories of Jesus underscore the close relationship among Christian and Jewish storytellers and, presumably, the close relationship among members of their religio-ethnic communities. At the same time, the extent of polemical elements reflects attempts by partisan storytellers to keep members of their respective religio-ethnic communities appropriately separate from the other.[6]

The variety, episodic similarities, and the polemical functions of Christian and Jewish stories of Jesus prove to be a combination that is far too vast to treat in any amount of detail in a single paper. Here, I have confined my scope to a pared down version of two related, but limited, lines of inquiry. Section I outlines the early development of a specific subset of stories of Jesus—so-called "infancy" stories—in late antiquity. Collectively, these relate information about Jesus' parentage, conception, and childhood. Section II discusses the evolution of antique infancy stories of Jesus in medieval Europe and suggests ways that historical context may have informed regional developments. Doing so provides greater understanding of the complex relationships among Christians and Jews living in constant contact, and often conflict, in Northern Europe during the Middle Ages.

---

[6] In *Dying for God*, noted above, Daniel Boyarin has explored a similar phenomenon among early rabbis and priests who attempted to delineate their communities. In contrast to the "top-down" model he emphasizes as a reason for the ultimate severing of Jewish-Christian communities, the widespread diffusion of apocrypha and *Toledot Yeshu* in oral and written form suggests that divisions may have been propagated by community members rather than exclusively communal leaders. Below, I discuss how the specific polemical turn of apocrypha and *Toledot Yeshu* reflects the sentiments of anti-assimilationist partisans who were opposed to inter-confessional association.

I. The Early Development of Infancy Stories of Jesus in Late Antiquity

A. Canonical Christian Infancy Stories of Jesus

The most famous late antique stories of Jesus are those that arose in Jewish-Christian communities and would eventually[7] be included in two of the four Gospels of the Christian New Testament—the late first-century Gospel of Luke and the first- or second-century Gospel of Matthew.[8] While these are probably familiar to most readers, a review will be helpful when comparing extra-canonical and non-Christian stories of Jesus.

Luke's account, composed in a variety of Greek forms,[9] is, by far, the more detailed of the two and provides the lion's share of details popularly associated with Jesus' conception and early life. This Gospel begins with a chapter detailing the divinely ordained conception of John the Baptist by Elizabeth and Zechariah, cousin and cousin-in-law, respectively, of Jesus' mother, Mary. The placement of this introductory infancy story of John functions sequentially to reinforce Luke's text: a prophet (John) came before the Messiah (Jesus), in order that he might "prepare his ways, to give knowledge of salvation to his people" (Lk. 1:76-7). Luke's first chapter also establishes that Mary came from an especially devout family (Zechariah was a priest and Elizabeth was descended from the priestly lineage of Aaron, brother of Moses) who had experienced God's miraculous involvement in domestic affairs.[10] As such, it was less of a surprise when the Gospel

---

[7] On the premise that the infancy segments were written later than the other portions of the Gospels, see Marina Warner, *Alone of All Her Sex: The Myth and the Cult of the Virgin Mary* (New York: Vintage Books, 1983), 4.

[8] For the dating of the Gospels, see Michael D. Coogan, et al., ed., introduction to the Gospel of Matthew and the Gospel of Luke, in *The New Oxford Annotated Bible*, 3rd ed. (Oxford: Oxford University Press, 2007), 7-8, 94. Incidentally, the above edition of *The New Oxford Annotated Bible* is the biblical text cited throughout this essay.

[9] Coogan, et al. *Oxford Annotated Bible*, 93.

[10] Lk. 1:5.

relates the angel Gabriel's Annunciation to Mary that God had chosen her to conceive Heaven's son, Jesus. When Mary questioned how this could happen, not least of all, because she was a virgin—a characteristic mentioned twice in Luke 1:27—Gabriel told her: "The Holy Spirit will come upon you, and the power of the Most High will overshadow you; therefore the child to be born will be holy; he will be called Son of God" (Lk. 1:35). And Mary consented.

Luke continues by providing an account of Jesus' hasty Nativity in a manger, occurring on the way to Bethlehem where the family was traveling to register for the Roman census; Jesus' circumcision and presentation at the Temple; and, when he was bit older, a twelve-year-old Jesus teaching at the Temple.[11] As an accompaniment to these familiar events and Jewish rites of passage, Luke strategically includes affirmations by Jews that Jesus was the awaited Messiah of Israel and thus indicates that the child's identity was recognized early on by pious members of the Jewish community. For example, when a recently pregnant Mary went to visit her cousin, Elizabeth immediately knew that Jesus—even in utero—was the fulfillment of Hebrew prophecy of God's promised Messiah: "When Elizabeth heard Mary's greeting, the child leaped in her womb. And Elizabeth was filled with the Holy Spirit and exclaimed with a loud cry, 'Blessed are you among women ... the mother of my Lord ...'" (Lk. 1:41-3). An angel revealed to shepherds tending their flocks the night Jesus was born that the child was "a Savior, who is the Messiah" (Lk. 2:11) and inspired them to adore the infant. The prophetess Anna, who lived at the Temple at the time of Jesus' presentation, spoke "about the child to all who were looking for the redemption of Jerusalem" (Lk. 2:39). And a devout layman, Simeon, who was "looking forward to the consolation of Israel" (Lk. 2:25) and who was also in attendance at Jesus' presentation, recognized through the aid of the Holy Spirit that he had seen the "Lord's Messiah." (Lk. 2:26) This knowledge prompted Simeon to warn Mary that Jesus would be both accepted and denied by many in Israel, and that she herself would be caught in

---

[11] See Lk. 2.

the crossfire of her son's message: "This child is destined for the falling and the rising of many in Israel ... and a sword will pierce your own soul too" (Lk. 2:34).

Luke's structure and tropes are somewhat similar to those found in Matthew. As in Luke, Matthew's infancy segment is composed of two short chapters that herald Jesus' impressive human ancestry, attempt to establish Jesus as the fulfillment of Hebrew messianic prophecy, and highlight Mary's miraculous Virgin Birth of Jesus. Beyond these elements, the information and emphases found in the infancy stories of the two Gospels differs. For example, Matthew's genealogy of Jesus complements rather than echoes Luke's. Whereas Luke opens with a discussion of Mary's family's priestly and prophetic lineage before going on to discuss the Annunciation, Nativity, etc., Matthew begins with a detailed lineage of Joseph that stretches back in four segments of fourteen to include such notable persona and moments in Judaic tradition as the patriarch Abraham, the messianic king, David, and the Babylonian Exile: "Thus there were fourteen generations in all from Abraham to David, fourteen from David to the exile to Babylon, and fourteen from the exile to the Messiah" (Mt. 1: 17). Scholars have conjectured that Matthew may have originally been composed in Hebrew, and have shown that Matthew's repetition of the number of generations—fourteen—was intended to invoke for his Hebrew-speaking audience the numerical equivalent of David's name, thus providing further evidence that Jesus was the "son" (descendant) of the messianic King David, and the awaited Messiah in his own right.[12]

Only after tracing Jesus' patrilineal heritage does Matthew provide information regarding Joseph's reaction to discovering his fiancée pregnant and the events that followed: "When his [Jesus'] mother Mary had been engaged to Joseph, but before they lived together, she was found to be with child" (Mt. 1:18). Joseph initially thought of dismissing Mary, albeit quietly, until the Lord appeared to him in a

---

[12] Coogan, et al. Oxford Annotated Bible, 9; James E. Patrick, "Matthew's Pesher Gospel Structured around Ten Messianic Citations of Isaiah," *The Journal of Theological Studies*, New Series, 61, no. 1 (2010): 63.

dream and told him that the child was conceived by the Holy Spirit. And "When Joseph awoke from sleep, he did as the angel of the Lord commanded him; he took her [Mary] as his wife, but had no marital relations with her until she had borne a son; and he named him Jesus" (Mt. 1:24-5).

According to Matthew, shortly after the Nativity, King Herod was alerted to the birth of a political rival by three magi, wisemen from the East, who came searching for him to show their respects. The magi had followed a star which they believed announced the birth of the "king of the Jews," (Mt. 2:2) and they asked Herod where they might find the child. Jealous Herod thought to trick the wisemen into finding and telling him where the child was so that he might slay him. Though the magi succeeded on their quest, Herod's plan failed; the travelers did not return to tell the temperamental ruler the location of the child, for they had been warned in a dream to avoid him. Angered that his plot had been foiled, Herod ordered the slaughter of all male Israelite children under the age of two in what would come to be known as the "Massacre of the Innocents." Like the magi, Joseph had been warned in a dream to flee Bethlehem with his family and hide from Herod in Egypt. When Herod died and the threat of imminent danger had passed, Joseph had another dream vision in which the angel of the Lord told him to return to Galilee with his family.[13]

Matthew's recurring theme of Joseph's reception of revelatory dreams is reminiscent of the earlier Hebrew dreamer of the same name, Joseph, son of Abraham, who accepted the responsibility of providing for the material needs of Israel before and during the nation's sojourn in Egypt.[14] In further connection to Judaic tradition,

---

[13] See Mt. 2: 3-22.
[14] See Warner, *Alone of All Her Sex*, 6. Matthew's association of a biblical name with specific characteristics (i.e., visionary capabilities, provider, etc.) has a long history in the Judaic exegetical tradition of *pesher*. This tradition was en vogue among messianic and apocalyptic sects at the time Matthew wrote his Gospel and, recently, James E. Patrick has argued for several other instances of *pesher* in the Gospel of Matthew. See Patrick, "Matthew's Pesher Gospel," 43-81.

Matthew includes a number of quotations, also known as prooftexts,[15] from the Hebrew Bible and contemporary messianic literature in efforts to effectively illustrate that Jesus was in fact the fulfillment of Hebrew prophecy and the awaited Messiah of Israel. The first of these is found near the conclusion of Matthew's genealogy, immediately after Gabriel tells Joseph in a dream to take Mary as a wife, despite her condition: "All this took place to fulfill what had been spoken by the Lord through the prophet: 'Look, the virgin shall conceive and bear a son, and they shall name him Emmanuel,' which means, 'God is with us'" (Mt. 1:22-3).

The prooftext here—"Look, the virgin shall conceive ... "—is based on a revised version of the authoritative Greek translation of Hebrew Scripture, the Septuagint, that the Gospel writer employed and, most likely, adjusted his narrative to match.[16] The verse it alludes to is found in the messianic prophecy of Isaiah: "Look, the young woman is with child and shall bear a son, and shall name him Immanuel" (Is. 7:14). The Hebrew term for young woman (of a marriageable age), *'almah*, was inconsistently translated in the Septuagint as either young woman or virgin.[17] The use of the Greek term, *parthenos*, virgin, for the Hebrew, *'almah*, became a key point in Luke and Matthew, as well as in later Christian doctrine discussed further below. The Gospel writers may have favored this translation because it was what they were most familiar with. At the same time, however, their accounts of Mary's virginal conception and birth of Jesus also coincided with popular contemporary Hellenistic stories of

---

[15] Prooftexts are quotations from—or sometimes allusions to—authoritative religious literature that are used to argue (i.e., prove) a point. Within the Judaic tradition, authoritative religious literature might include quotations from the Hebrew Bible, talmudic literature, commentary by esteemed rabbis, and more.

[16] See Maarten J. J. Menken, "The Textual Form of the Quotation from Isaiah 7:14 in Matthew 1:23," *Novum Testamentum* 43, no 2 (2001): 144-60, especially 147-55.

[17] Warner, *Alone of All Her Sex*, 19.

demigods and heroes who were born of virgins.[18] Thus, it is possible that the common trope was intended to help Christians ingratiate Jesus to pagans in the same way that references from the Hebrew Bible were employed to convince Jews of his messiahship. But if this was a calculated move, the plan backfired. For Jews, pagans, and every other group of non-believers seemed to have found particular delight in mocking the doctrines of the Virgin Birth and Incarnation, and in watching Christians perform mental acrobatics to defend them. This is most blatant in the Jewish rumors that would find their way into rabbinic literature and, later, in the full-blown stories about Jesus that circulated among Jewish communities throughout the world.

B. Jewish Infancy Stories of Jesus (According to Jews, Pagans, and Christians)

There are no extant Jewish infancy stories of Jesus from late antiquity.[19] There are, however, hints peppered throughout rabbinic literature that versions may have existed in the first centuries of the Common Era, perhaps in oral form. A number of clues are also found in polemical writings by early Christians. These include second- and sometimes third-hand snippets of antagonistic Jewish infancy stories of Jesus that mock the doctrines of the Virgin Birth and Incarnation. Though originating in the hands of Christians, the latter category cannot be written off as mere hearsay. Instead, the similarities between Jewish and Christian references reflect what has been the growing consensus

---

[18] Warner, *Alone of All Her Sex*, 34-5. The literary introduction of Luke also resembles Hellenistic histories, especially. See Coogan, et al. *Oxford Annotated Bible*, 95.

[19] The earliest versions of the *Toledot Yeshu* are believed to have circulated orally in the antique Levant and there is some evidence to suggest a compositional date of the fourth or fifth century CE, though this remains debated. See Pierluigi Piovanelli, "The Toledot Yeshu and Christian Apocryphal Literature: The Formative Years," in *Toledot Yeshu ("The Life Story of Jesus") Revisited: A Princeton Conference*, ed. Peter Schäfer, Michael Meerson, and Yaacov Deutsch, Texts and Studies in Ancient Judaism 143 (Tübingen: Mohr Siebeck, 2011), 94.

among scholars of religion and history—namely, that early Christian and Jewish communities were very much in contact with one another, if not part of a single community, who sought definition (individual and collective identity) through opposition.[20]

Recent scholarship of Jewish traditions about Jesus found in the late antique rabbinic corpus suggests the existence of deliberate counter narratives to the canonical Gospel accounts of Jesus' conception, life, and death.[21] These may have been part of already formulated Jewish stories of Jesus that either existed solely in oral form or that have not been preserved, for one reason or another. At the very least, there is no doubt that stray rabbinic comments would contribute to the majority of the later, full-fledged Jewish counter narratives—the *Toledot Yeshu*.

Rabbinic accounts, including information pertinent to Jewish infancy stories of Jesus, aim to refute the doctrines of the Virgin Birth and Incarnation by mentioning the activities and/or moral character of his very human parents—especially his mother, Mary.[22] In one Talmudic tradition, Mary had a husband, Stada, along with her Roman lover known only by the exceedingly common name, Pandera (or Panthera), and Jesus could have been the son of either. In another, Mary's husband's name was Pappos ben Yehudah and he would lock her in the house every time he left in the hopes of maintaining her wifely chastity. Pappos' lack of success is suggested by the term "Stada," here a reference to Mary's extra-marital activity as a *sotah*, or adulteress, who engaged in illicit relations with the Roman soldier Pandera.[23] In related Talmudic traditions alluding to promiscuity, Mary is said to have occupied herself as a spinner of cloth who let her

---

[20] Again, see Boyarin, *Dying for God*; idem, *Border Lines*.

[21] Peter Schäfer, *Jesus in the Talmud* (Princeton: Princeton University Press, 2007), 8-9, 15, 122, 129.

[22] Jesus' name is not specified in the following passages. However, because the same patrilineal (ben Pandera, son of Pandera) is intertextually applied to Jesus, it is a fair assumption. For a concise review of such references, see Schäfer, *Jesus in the Talmud*, 133-43.

[23] Schäfer, *Jesus in the Talmud*, 15-22; idem, "Jesus' Origin, Birth, and Childhood according to the *Toledot Yeshu* and the Talmud," in *Judaea-Palaestina, Babylon and Rome: Jews in Antiquity*, ed. Benjamin Isaac and

"women's hair grow long" and left it uncovered in public, suggesting a lack of modesty and that she may have been plying more than her handiwork at market.[24]

Christians were well aware of Jewish critiques. The second-century Christian apologist Justin Martyr (d. 165) wrote a good deal about them in his polemical treatise, *Dialogue with Trypho*. As the title suggests, this text presents an account of Justin's conversations with Trypho, a Jew. The subject of their conversation: the finer points of religious doctrine. The dialogic form of Justin's *Dialogue* is a commonplace in philosophical treatises aimed at refuting the belief systems of others and most likely does not record an actual conversation that the author had with a Jew named Trypho. It does, however, provide a relatively thorough model of how Christians might respond to a myriad of Jewish doctrinal criticisms. As such, it suggests the types of arguments contemporary Jews leveled at their Christian neighbors or, at the very least, Christian self-consciousness at doctrinal elements that Jews might deride with some sting of validity. These include explicit acknowledgment that Jews did not approve of the translation of *'almah* that Matthew and Luke employed as an integral component of the Isaiah 7:14 prooftext cited for the messiahship of Jesus, and a pointed comparison of the Christian doctrines of the Virgin Birth and Incarnation with Greek mythology.[25]

Early Christian knowledge of Jewish critiques went well beyond linguistic and tropic similarity, though. In *Althēs Logos*, Word of Truth (ca. 177)—a text by the second-century pagan philosopher Celsus that has been preserved only in quotation by the Church Father Origen in his treatise, *Contra Celsum*, Against Celsus (ca. 231-33)—a Jewish character relates his community's belief that Jesus was the product of an adulterous liaison between Mary and a certain Roman

---

    Yuval Shahar (Tübingen: Mohr Siebeck, 2012), 141-43; and Meerson and Schäfer, introduction to *Toledot Yeshu*, 46-7.

[24] Schäfer, *Jesus in the Talmud*, 17-18; and Meerson and Schäfer, introduction to *Toledot Yeshu*, 46.

[25] Justin Martyr, *Dialogue with Trypho*, ed. Michael Slusser, trans. Thomas B. Falls (Washington D.C.: The Catholic University Press, 2003), 66, 102-04.

soldier identified only as Pandera. When Mary's husband discovered the affair, he drove her away and, as a result, she led a life of poverty as a spinner of cloth.[26] In a contemporary treatise *De spectaculis*, On Spectacles (ca. 200), the Christian author Tertullian provided a brief comment on Jewish belief in regard to Mary that was, perhaps, even less flattering: Jesus was *quaestuariae filius*, a "prostitute's son."[27]

The Church Father Jerome's *Epistola ad Titum*, Letter to Titus (ca. 400), suggests that Jewish criticism of the Christian doctrines of the Virgin Birth and Incarnation were not merely literary, for it provides an account of Roman Jews who disturbed the peace by continuing to pose agitating questions regarding Jesus' parentage into the fifth century.[28] And the eighth-century *Vita Silvestri*, Life of St. Sylvester, likewise depicts sustained Jewish incredulity of Mary's virginal-maternal status in a public disputation.[29] The sections below discuss how early Christian apocrypha either responded to or anticipated some of these insults.

C. Early Apocryphal Stories of Jesus: The Infancy Gospels of James and Thomas

Luke's and Matthew's canonical infancy stories of Jesus are but two among many Christian versions to originate and circulate in the late antique Levantine and Mediterranean regions. As noted above, the Gospel accounts include Hellenistic tropes that would become doctrine, such as the Virgin Birth and Incarnation, while positioning Jesus' miraculous Nativity as a fulfillment of Hebrew messianic prophecy in a manner that might appeal to both pagan and Jewish audiences. In addition to these accounts, the apocrypha that did not make it into the cannon would continue to be transmitted by word of mouth, in writing, and through iconography, spreading to far-

---

[26] Schäfer, *Jesus in the Talmud*, 18-20.
[27] Schäfer, *Jesus in the Talmud*, 112; Meerson and Schäfer, introduction to *Toledot Yeshu*, 6-7, 45.
[28] Meerson and Schäfer, introduction to *Toledot Yeshu*, 5-6.
[29] Meerson and Schäfer, introduction to *Toledot Yeshu*, 5-6.

flung regions and continuing to evolve long after their first iterations. Indeed, many apocryphal traditions remain significant to Christians around the world in the modern era.[30]

Part of the reason for the apocrypha's longevity is that popular stories about Jesus and the Holy Family have been told right alongside or even instead of the official Gospel accounts since the early centuries of Christianity's development.[31] The New Testament canon was not closed until the sixth century.[32] Thus the stories that would come to be known as the apocrypha, like the Gospel accounts, originated among early Christians who were formulating and propagating their beliefs about their savior without the benefit, or constriction, of later-developed official doctrine. Their continued spread after the closing of the canon is best understood within the context of multiple Christian sects and disputes regarding orthodox and heterodox (or heretical) teaching throughout antiquity and the Middle Ages—namely, that doctrinal diffusion, acceptance, and supersession among Christians who cherished different beliefs and traditions was a long time coming.

Popularity might also be owing to the fact that apocrypha are often shorter and their message simpler, serving to reinforce or contribute to Church teachings rather than introduce new ones altogether.[33] Additionally, it may be the case that, because stories unbound by the canon were free to evolve on the lips and pens of their tellers, the apocrypha better responded to their audience's context in a way that the Gospels did not. These later scenarios are evidenced in two of the

---

[30] This is especially the case with apocrypha that has been incorporated into hagiography and later Church practice, such as the Stations of the Cross/ *Via Dolorosa* traditions associated with St. Veronica.

[31] For a thorough discussion of the apocrypha in relation to the New Testament, see Bart D. Ehrman, *Lost Christianities: The Battles for Scripture and the Faith We Never Knew* (New York: Oxford University Press, 2003).

[32] Dale B. Martin, *New Testament History and Literature* (New Haven: Yale University Press, 2012), 27.

[33] The majority of Christian tradition regarding Joseph, Mary, and Mary's parents is from the apocrypha and apocryphal iconography. See Carlidge and Elliott, *Art and the Christian Apocrypha*, 21-3.

most popular ancient apocryphal texts: The *Infancy Gospel of James* and the *Infancy Gospel of Thomas*.

The *Infancy Gospel of James* is believed to have been composed by a pseudonymous Jewish- Christian author,[34] writing in koine, in Greek-speaking Egypt, sometime between 180 and 200.[35] Though it provides information about the Annunciation and Nativity of Jesus, the *Infancy Gospel of James* is more aptly described as an account of Mary's life. The fullest versions of the text begin with the embarrassment of infertility suffered by Mary's pious, wealthy, and aging parents, Joachim and Anna, until an angel of the Lord appeared and announced to both that they would be blessed with a child.[36] Joachim and Anna dedicated Mary to the Lord in gratitude and, on her third birthday, took her to be raised at the Temple among the undefiled virgin daughters of Israel. Toddler Mary danced with joy at her presentation before the priest and high altar, where she was blessed as a singular revealer of redemption and was said to be loved by all of Israel. She was also loved by Heaven, for as she grew in God's house she was alleged to have been fed from angelic hands.

---

[34] Though the author's identity remains unknown, their ethnicity is often assumed to be Jewish due to the extensive use of the Septuagint. See Harm R. Smid, *Protevangelium Jacobi: A Commentary*, Apocrypha Novi Testament 1 (Assen: van Gorcum, 1965); E. Cothenet, "Le Protévangile de Jacques: origine, genre et signification d'un premier midrash chrétien sur la Nativité de Marie," *Aufstieg und Niedergang der römischen Welt* 2.25.6 (1988): 4252-69. As noted below, I believe that the author was also familiar with rabbinic literature. Even so, some scholars have recently begun to question the author's Jewish identity. See Ronald F. Hock, *The Infancy Gospels of James and Thomas*, The Scholars Bible (Santa Rosa, CA: Polebridge Press, 1995), 9-10.

[35] Pamela Sheingorn, "Reshaping of the Childhood Miracles of Jesus," in *The Christ Child in Medieval Culture: Alpha es et O!*, ed. Mary Dzon and Theresa M. Kenney (Toronto: University of Toronto Press, 2012), 256.

[36] I have consulted the version translated by Ronald F. Hock in *The Infancy Gospels*, 32-77, with the exception of the presentation of Joseph's staff in Chapter 9, for which I have consulted Cartlidge and Elliott, *Art and the Christian Apocrypha*, 24-5. See note 39 below.

Despite these honors, when she reached the age of twelve, Mary's story took an abrupt turn. The priests, probably fearful of the impending onset of adolescence, menstruation, and subsequent defilement of the Temple,[37] decided that she should be cared for by a widower of Israel who would be identified by a sign from Heaven. Joseph's election was indicated by the sudden blossoming of his staff.[38] And so, despite his misgivings, Joseph took Mary in before promptly leaving on business. During Joseph's absence, Mary occupied her time by sewing a portion of the Temple curtain at the behest of the priests. With this occupational detail, James' gospel responds to, and attempts to subvert, Jewish and pagan polemic that Mary spun cloth out of necessity and in shame because Joseph had left her. In further contrast to the polemical accounts, James' gospel indicates that Mary's work preceded an angelic visit from Gabriel and the Annunciation that she had been chosen to conceive the Lord's child. Shortly thereafter, as in the Gospel of Luke, Mary visited her

---

[37] The treatment of menstruant women, *niddah*, in Jewish law suggests that Mary's imminent puberty was the underlying concern of the priests' eagerness to see her leave the Temple at the age of 12. For biblical stipulations regarding *niddah*, see Lev. 15:19-33. For a treatment of menstruation in Greek sacred texts, see S. G. Cole, "*Gynaikiou Themis*: Gender Difference in the Greek *Leges Sacrae*," *Helios* 19 (1992): 104-22, especially 111. For a discussion of antique rabbinic treatment of *niddah*, see Alexandra Cuffel, *Gendering Disgust in Medieval Religious Polemic* (Notre Dame: University of Notre Dame Press, 2007), 32-5.

[38] The detail of Joseph's blossoming staff was most common in the Byzantine cycle of the Life of the Virgin, though it was known in Western Europe and represented in Western iconography. See Cartlidge and Elliott, *Art and the Christian Apocrypha*, 24-5. In other versions of the text, the sign of Joseph's election entailed a dove emerging from the widower's staff. See Hock, *The Infancy Gospels*, 49; Ehrman, *Lost Scriptures*, 66. The sexual connotation of the dove—an ancient fertility symbol representing the Holy Spirit and recognized as the generative person of the Trinity in the Gospel of Luke (Lk. 1:35)—emerging from the phallic staff of Joseph is rich here. Perhaps the double entendre is why the staff with a dove alighting was a less popular iconographic representation of Jesus' stepfather's election.

pregnant cousin Elizabeth who immediately knew, and proclaimed, that she was pregnant with her Lord.

When Mary returned home, Joseph's initial reaction upon discovering the Temple virgin pregnant was less welcoming—until, that is, an angelic dream vision revealed that she was carrying God's child, as in Matthew's Gospel. After this vision, Joseph defended Mary when her virginity was questioned by a scribe and a priest of the Temple who put their testimony to the test in a trial by ordeal that entailed the drinking of foul, brackish water, and traveling to the wilderness alone to see if God would, essentially, preserve the pious or smote the sinners. When both Mary and Joseph returned healthy, the priest conceded their blamelessness before God but, evidently, it was not known throughout Israel. For Mary's honor would by questioned again at the Nativity.

While she was in childbed in a cave, en route to Bethlehem for the Roman census, Joseph sought out a Hebrew midwife to attend Mary. The midwife remained in disbelief until awed by a miraculous light from Heaven. After blessing the family, the midwife went away and told an acquaintance, Salome, whom she met along the road, of the night's events. This second Hebrew midwife was audacious enough to perform a gynecological examination to determine if Mary was in fact a virgin mother. As divine retribution for this act of temerity, Salome's hand withered until she prayed to God for forgiveness and obediently held the baby Jesus to attest to his divinity. The text goes on to describe the adoration of the magi before closing with events surrounding the "Massacre of the Innocents." Here, shortly after the magi departed to avoid Herod, Mary—rather than Joseph, as in Matthew's account—learned of the ruler's murderous plot. Fearing for the safety of her child, she wrapped him in swaddling clothes and put him in a manger to hide him before the Holy Family fled to Egypt. The text closes with description of how Elizabeth too feared for her son, John the Baptist. When she could not travel to safety because of her age and fragility, God opened a mountain to receive them both as Herod's henchmen murdered her husband for his refusal to help locate his child who was also of the condemned age.

The *Infancy Gospel of James* shares a number of narrative elements with Luke and Matthew to an extent that suggests the authors of all three accounts may have based their versions on an older, more encompassing infancy story. This also suggests that James sought to answer questions—and polemical criticisms of inconsistency—arising from reading alternative accounts.[39] More extensively than Luke, James focusses on Mary's lineage and familial relationships to her parents and cousin, Elizabeth, as well as the census precipitating the birth of Jesus. However, like Matthew, James also includes specific details that are lacking in Luke—such as Joseph's proclivity to receive divine revelations while dreaming. Perhaps more pertinently, the *Infancy Gospel of James* also shares and expands upon the themes of the Virgin Birth, Incarnation, and the idea that Jesus represented a fulfillment of God's messianic promise to redeem Israel that contemporary Jews and pagans mocked. Each of these details would become especially important in the development of Christian doctrine and its defense against polemical attacks.

The canonical accounts of the Virgin Birth, uttered by the narrators and angel Gabriel in Matthew and Luke, were effectually verified by the added scenario of the priestly trial by ordeal of Mary and Joseph in James' account. Both the Virgin Birth and the Incarnation were also validated beyond events described in the Gospels regarding the Nativity—namely, by the heavenly light viewed by the first midwife and by Salome's affliction and subsequent healing as a reward for obediently showing due deference to the Christ child. Written against the backdrop of Jewish and pagan rumors of her promiscuity,[40] the emphasis on Mary's overall purity, and especially her virginity, suggests that her intact hymen was a defining characteristic. In time, it seems, the apocrypha impacted doctrine. For the idea that Mary remained a virgin perpetually and not just "*until* she had borne a son"

---

[39] J. K. Elliott, *The Apocryphal New Testament: A Collection of Apocryphal Christian Literature in an English Translation Based on M. R. James* (Oxford: Clarendon Press, 1993), 50; Hock, *The Infancy Gospels*, 23.

[40] Scholars have commonly interpreted the *Infancy Gospel of James* as an apologetic account. In contrast to the consensus, see Hock, *The Infancy Gospels*, 15-20.

(Mt. 1:25), became widely supported by Christian exegetes as early as the fourth century. It would later become the official Church position and was determined significant enough to reaffirm in the catechism at the Council of Trent (1545-63).[41]

Finally, while Luke emphasizes Jewish rites of passage surrounding Jesus' early childhood, such as circumcision and presentation at the Temple, and Matthew extensively utilizes prooftexts to illustrate that Jesus was the fulfillment of God's messianic promise to Israel, James' account employs a combination of references to the Temple cult as well as biblical and rabbinic writings to the same end. James' presentation and the later popular iconographic representation of Joseph's flowering staff that signaled his election as Mary's protector,[42] for instance, alludes to the biblical account of Aaron's staff that blossomed as a sign of election to the priesthood.[43] Rabbinic traditions composed in the first centuries of the Common Era conflate Aaron's staff with that of Moses' and describe it as a wonder-working instrument that had been wielded since the days of Adam but had subsequently been hidden until the time of the Messiah. Upon his arrival, such texts assure, the Messiah would use the staff's power to redeem Israel.[44] The concept of dual messianic figures (a lesser messianic precursor to a greater redeemer figure), one of whom was hidden until the time of redemption is another trope familiar within rabbinic and Jewish messianic traditions.[45]

---

[41] Warner, *Alone of All Her Sex*, 43-5.
[42] Cartlidge and Elliott, *Art and the Christian Apocrypha*, 25-6.
[43] See Nm. 17:8.
[44] See Louis Ginzberg, *The Legends of the Jews*, vol. 6 (Philadelphia: Jewish Publication Society, 1909-38), 6:106-7; Christine Meilicke, "Moses' Staff and the Return of the Dead," *Jewish Studies Quarterly* 6 (1999): 347; John C. Reeves, *Trajectories in Near Eastern Apocalyptic: A Postrabbinic Jewish Apocalypse Reader* (Atlanta: Society of Biblical Literature, 2005), 188-89.
[45] For an overview of the concept of an occluded Messiah, see Martha Himmelfarb, "The Mother of the Messiah in the Talmud Yerushalmi and Sefer Zerubbabel," in *The Talmud Yerushalmi and Graeco-Roman Culture*, ed. Peter Schäfer, Texts and Studies in Ancient Judaism 93 (Tübingen: Mohr Siebeck, 2002), 369-89, especially 376-78.

These few examples indicate that the authors of the canonical Gospels and James' account hoped to appeal to Hellenistic Jews by legitimizing the Holy Family through contemporary and traditional Judaic customs and literature while defending them from persistent polemical attacks. By insinuating that Mary, her family, and Joseph were Jews *par excellence* who affirmed the advent of the Christian Messiah, James' account functioned as an attempt to establish their intermediary positions between the "Old" covenant of Judaism and the "New" covenant of Christ.[46] Yet, at the same time, James' memorable presentation of Salome provides an interesting dichotomy that recurs time and again in the history of Jewish-Christian relations—namely, a tentative license for violence against non-believers juxtaposed to an example of magnanimous forgiveness and restoration. This conveys the idea that Jewish converts, however late in coming, were welcome into the fold of the Church.

The same backhanded welcome would be echoed in official Church policy of toleration articulated by Church Father, Augustine of Hippo (354-430), when he called for Christians to permit Jews to live among them and not to harm them.[47] His admonition was based on the belief that Christ's return would only be realized once the majority of Jews finally accepted Jesus as the long-awaited Messiah by converting to Christianity of their own accord.[48] By contrast, the condoning of

---

[46] Cartlidge and Elliott, *Art and the Christian Apocrypha*, 23, assign the role of "bridge," or intermediary, between Judaism and Christianity to Mary. In James' account, this function appears to be shared among members of the extended Holy Family: Joachim, Anna, Elizabeth, Zechariah, Mary, and Joseph.

[47] Augustine, *The City of God*, 18.46 in *The City of God, Books XVII-XXII*, trans. Gerald G. Walsh and Daniel J. Honan, The Fathers of the Church 24 (Washington, DC: The Catholic University of America, 1954), 164-65.

[48] There are varied schools of thought regarding the reach of Augustinian tolerance. A number of scholars have approached the topic from a materialist perspective and have pointed out that the tenet of qualified toleration did not have a major impact in terms of socio-economic and political relationships between Jews and the leaders of various communities throughout the Latin West—that is to say, Jews were permitted to reside throughout different areas because of the benefits (usually economic) they provided to the local

violence against unbelieving Jews was largely frowned upon, at least among the highest ranking Church officials,[49] but would become

> ruler and not due to any reverence for Judaism, or in the hopes of successful proselytization. Likewise, when violence erupted against Jews, it was not an intended breach of an unrecognized or irrelevant Augustinian ideal. See, for instance, David Nirenberg, *Communities of Violence: Persecution of Minorities in the Middle Ages* (Princeton: Princeton University Press, 1996); Jonathan Elukin, *Living Together, Living Apart: Rethinking Jewish-Christian Relations in the Middle Ages* (Princeton: Princeton University Press, 2009); and Robert Chazan, *Reassessing Jewish Life in Medieval Europe* (Cambridge: Cambridge University Press, 2010). While these texts do make some valid points, they (especially Nirenberg's) are largely reactionary, written in response to R. I. Moore's sweeping, Foucauldian generalization of the medieval emergence of a bureaucratized web of intolerance in *The Formulation of a Persecuting Society: Authority and Deviance in Western Europe, 950-1250* (Oxford: Blackwell, 1987). For examples of those who do consider Augustinian tolerance to have had an impact on Jewish-Christian relations, see Gavin I. Langmuir, *Toward a Definition of Antisemitism* (Berkeley: University of California Press, 1990); and David E. Timmer "Biblical Exegesis and the Jewish-Christian Controversy in the Early Twelfth Century," *Church History* 58, no. 3 (1989): 309-21; and Anna Sapir Abulafia, *Christians and Jews in the Twelfth-Century Renaissance* (London: Routledge, 1995); these authors opine that the dissipation of Augustinian tolerance began to emerge with the rationalist turn during the long twelfth century, in which those attempting to effectively argue the supreme coherence of Christianity did so at the expense of Judaism and Jews. Jeremy Cohen has repeatedly claimed that Augustinian tolerance only truly began to dissolve in the thirteenth century via the polemics of the friars. See *The Friars and the Jews: The Evolution of Medieval Anti-Judaism* (Ithaca, NY: Cornell University Press, 1982); idem, "Scholarship and Intolerance in the Medieval Academy: The Study and Evaluation of Judaism in European Christendom," *American Historical Review* 91 (1986): 592-613; idem, *Living Letters of the Law: Ideas of the Jew in Medieval Christianity* (Berkeley and Los Angeles: University of California Press, 1999), 23 65. There is much to appreciate in these arguments; however, as the emergence of widespread anti-Jewish persecution occurred before the majority of intellectual justifications for it, one may deduce a somewhat earlier fomentation and a motivation other than heightened rationalism and rationalization. Vengeance—an explicit justification given in Latin and Hebrew narratives depicting pogroms—coincides with teachings of the Church in regard to Jewish culpability for Christ's crucifixion.

[49] See, for example, Friedrich Lotter, *Die Konzeption des Wendenkreuzzugs* (Sigmaringen: Thorbecke, 1977), 34-8.

all the more blatant in another popular apocryphal text, the *Infancy Gospel of Thomas*, and, in time, an increasingly frequent occurrence in Christian Northern Europe.

The *Infancy Gospel of Thomas* is a pseudonymous text believed to have been composed during the second century[50] in the Eastern half of the Roman Empire. Like James' account, it was originally written in koine,[51] and filled in some of the gaps found in the canonical Gospels. But meaningful similarities end here. Unlike James' account, it is not a continuous narrative but a collection of stories focussed exclusively on the miracles (or exploits, depending on the audience's perspective) of the young Jesus, aged roughly five to twelve, and thus bookended by the biblical account of the Holy Family's return from Egypt and Jesus teaching at the Temple. While there are a number of versions of Thomas' account that contain one or more different stories, the evident function of each is to underscore Jesus' divinity—the doctrine of the Incarnation. Common episodes include a young Jesus sculpting clay birds on the Sabbath and, when reprimanded for working during the period of rest, defiantly animating them and commanding them to fly away; Jesus killing one or more other children for spoiling his play, or vexing him for some other minor infraction, and Joseph reprimanding him; and Jesus cursing his teacher and rendering him incapacitated because the man had grown aggravated at difficult questioning and

---

[50] Some debate remains regarding the dating of the *Infancy Gospel of Thomas* because, as with the *Infancy Gospel of James*, only later manuscripts are extant. According to Stephen Gero, "The Infancy Gospel of Thomas: A Study of the Textual and Literary Problems," *Novum Testamentum* 13 (1971): 48, the earliest date from the fifth to sixth century. As a result, some scholars at the extremis propose that the *Infancy Gospel of Thomas* might not have been written until the sixth century but may have circulated in oral form much earlier. Regardless of the limited textual remains, the second century is generally accepted as the origin of this narrative. See Hock, *The Infancy Gospels*, 91-2; Ehrman, *Lost Scriptures*, 58; Sheingorn, "Reshaping of the Childhood Miracles," 257.

[51] Hock, *The Infancy Gospels*, 90-1.

slapped the head of the boy who so arrogantly displayed superior knowledge.[52]

In these stories, Jesus eventually heals those he harmed once they show contrition or the community threatens to ostracize the Holy Family, but he does so grudgingly and only as a result of public outcry and (usually) Joseph's admonishing entreats. As such, Thomas appears to have been less interested in affirming Jesus' (or Mary's) position as an intermediary between Covenants as proclaiming an ideology of the Christian supersession of Judaism and a model of violent suppression of Jews for an erstwhile pagan audience.[53] By casting Jesus as a hothead who engaged in violence towards irreverent Jews, these episodes appear to condone and even encourage Christian followers of Jesus to carry out similar acts. The section below discusses how this unofficial policy of anti-Jewish violence carried over into medieval apocrypha, and how Jews responded with more fully developed infancy stories of their own.

II. The Evolution of Infancy Stories of Jesus in Medieval Europe

A. Christian Infancy Apocrypha and Iconography

The *Infancy Gospel of James* and the *Infancy Gospel of Thomas* provided the basis for iconographic traditions and medieval apocrypha throughout the Christian world. The withered hand of Salome, Jesus and the birds, and Jesus rebuking his teacher(s) would become favorite scenes, prominently depicted in the stained glass of cathedral windows, on murals and frescoes, and in statuary and devotional objects.[54] (Jesus harming Jewish children was represented less frequently and, to my

---

[52] Each of these episodes is found in Chapters 2, 3, 4, 6-8, and in Ronald F. Hock's translation of the version of the *Infancy Gospel of Thomas* known as "Tischendorf A," in *The Infancy Gospels*, 104-43.
[53] See Sheingorn, "Reshaping of the Childhood Miracles," 277-9, 287.
[54] See Cartlidge and Elliott, *Art and the Christian Apocrypha*, 90, 107-8, 116.

knowledge, only within the manuscript tradition.[55]) Iconographic representations were owing to artists' familiarity with James' and Thomas' Greek infancy gospels, gleaned especially in Mediterranean workshops.[56] But the ubiquity in Continental Europe was also due to the evolution of these gospels in different contexts.

In Continental Europe, a popular hybrid of James' narrative and a version of Thomas' collection of stories (the *pars altera*) emerged during the seventh century in a text that would come to be known as the *Gospel of Pseudo-Matthew*. By the eighth century, Latin translations circulated throughout Europe, some of which reduced the role of Joseph to that of an unnecessary nag while casting Jesus as Mary's true protector and provider. This shift is representative of a minor motif of the doctrine of Christian supersessionism already present in Thomas' collection in which Joseph, a Jewish man, symbolizes adherence to the "Old Covenant" of Judaism and the Jewish people writ large.

As early as the sixth century, related but decidedly more polemical articulations of this model began to crop up in miracle stories of the Virgin Mary popularized by Gregory of Tours (c. 538-95) in his *De gloria martyrum* (the Glory of Martyrs), and reiterated in dozens of later texts to circulate throughout Continental Europe and the British Isles. In an especially popular story—the tale of the "Jewish Boy"—a Jewish youth was attracted to Christianity and visited a church where he partook of Holy Communion. When his father discovered the offense, he stoked the fire and threw his son in to kill him as punishment for committing an act that Jews considered to be idolatrous. The Virgin Mary miraculously protected the child while the townspeople answered the wailing of the boy's mother and rescued

---

[55] See, for example, *Gesta Infantiae Salvatoris*, Oxford, Bodleian Library, MS Selden Supra 38, f. 9r, ff. 22v-23r, in which Jesus is depicted killing a child who disrupted the pools he had created to make the clay for his birds, and is shown to have turned Jewish children into swine when their parents tried to hide them so that Jesus could not play with them. The conversion of Jewish children into "Christian" animals is a topic that deserves more treatment than possible in the current essay.

[56] Cartlidge and Elliott, *Art and the Christian Apocrypha*, 26.

them both. Mother and child were easily converted and welcomed into the Church; but the obstinate, abusive fool of a father who clung overmuch to Judaism was killed in the fire he had prepared for his son.[57]

B. Ashkenazic *Toledot Yeshu*

The first references to Jewish infancy stories about Jesus that suggest a written tradition (beyond the smattering of comments found in the rabbinic literature and pagan and Christian hearsay) emerged in Northern Europe more than two centuries after the introduction of the "Jewish Boy," and about a century after the Latin translation of *Gospel of Pseudo-Matthew* had begun to circulate. Earlier Levantine versions of *Toledot Yeshu* existed, to be sure, but these were more interested in Jesus' adult ministry and the events leading up to his death. Mention of the Jesus' birth and childhood are absent in these (the only allusion to his conception is the epithet "ben/bar Pandera," the son of Pandera).[58] These casually recall the ancient rumor that Jesus was the son of a Roman soldier in such a way as to suggest that the matter was already widely accepted and needed no further explanation. After all, not only Jews but Roman luminaries had spread the polemical attack against the then upstart religion during the early centuries of the Common Era.

The later assertions about Jesus' parentage, conception, and childhood became topics of interest in Northern Europe under entirely different circumstances. By the early Middle Ages, Christianity was no longer novel in the Levantine and Mediterranean regions. After it had become the official religion of the Roman Empire during the fourth century, Christianity rapidly spread into the Germanic

---

[57]   See the discussion of the tale of the Jewish Boy and its popularity in Western Europe in Miri Rubin, *Gentile Tales: The Narrative Assault on Late Medieval Jews* (Philadelphia: University of Pennsylvania Press, 1999), 7-39; and in Ora Limor, "Mary and the Jews: Story, Controversy, and Testimony," *Historein* 6 (2006): 66.

[58]   Meerson and Schäfer, introduction to the *Toledot Yeshu*, 47.

Successor States where missionaries confronted many of the same questions about the doctrines of the Virgin Birth and Incarnation, questions posed by a skeptical populace that had frequently been converted at the point of a sword.[59] Gospel and apocryphal accounts of Jesus and the Holy Family functioned, in this context, in the same noted educational and entertaining capacities. But the apocrypha also helped to ease the conversionary process and establish a cohesive group identity, in part, by identifying a group of people—Jews—who remained stubborn and dangerous outsiders.

In the fullest versions of Northern European, or Ashkenazic *Toledot Yeshu*, Jews responded to their Christian neighbors' polemical characterization of members of their community and the implicit license to harm those who refused to convert to Christianity with their own polemical characterizations of Christians and a celebration of violence against the Virgin Mary. Through crass language and innuendo, Ashkenazic *Toledot Yeshu* worked to undermine the doctrines of the Virgin Birth and Incarnation while speaking to the precarious position of Jewish minorities in Christian Europe who might be tempted to assimilate and/or convert.

The earliest indication of an Ashkenazic *Toledot Yeshu* tradition, like the ancient polemic surrounding Jesus, reaches us second hand. Beginning in the ninth century, Charlemagne (768-814) invited Jews into his realm for the linguistic abilities, culture, and wealth it was rightly assumed that they would bring.[60] When the new group of Jewish emigres and local Christians confronted each other, members

---

[59] Severe indoctrination was something of a continuation of the violent, expedited manner of cultural hegemony reflected in the practice of conversion by conquest that many pagans in Saxony and in Avar territory, as well as Visigothic Christians living along the Spanish March, had experienced under the Carolingian rulers. See, for example, Cullen J. Chandler, "Heresy and Empire: The Role of the Adoptionist Controversy in Charlemagne's Conquest of the Spanish March," *The International History Review* 24, no. 3 (2002): 505-27.

[60] Aryeh Grabois, "The *Hebraica Veritas* and Jewish-Christian Intellectual Relations in the Twelfth Century," Speculum 50, no. 4 (1975): 615-16; Elukin, *Living Together, Living Apart*, 47.

of the upper echelons of society and many religious scholars interacted amicably.[61] But, in time, some Christians became suspicious of the political, economic, and social protection that secular rulers offered Jews whom they held responsible for Jesus' death.[62] For their part, some Jews were leery of accommodating the broader Christian culture because, in efforts to maintain amicable relations with their hosts, and because of pragmatic concerns for Jewish livelihood, some rabbis had become lenient (some would say, overly lenient) in their interpretations of *halakhah*, or Jewish law. Their willingness to accommodate the needs of their community and the wishes of their hosts impacted regulations regarding anything from the handling of ritually impure meat, or trading in the trappings of Christians religious ceremony, or crafting synagogues to look like Christian churches, to fraternizing with apostates and Christians for economically advantageous purposes.[63] It is in this context of renewed efforts by Christians and Jews to maintain religio-ethnic distinction in an atmosphere where the lines had blurred that we see a resurgence in doctrinal disputes centered on the Nativity and Incarnation of Jesus.

In the mid-ninth century, Amulo (841-52), a Carolingian Archbishop of Lyon, was angered with what he perceived as deferential treatment of Jews in the realm. In efforts to encourage stricter laws regulating Jewish behavior, he complained of the alleged beliefs of his neighbors. In his treatise, *Contra Judaeos*, Against the Jews, Amulo claimed that Jews were so confident of their position in the Frankish

---

[61] Grabois, "*Hebraica Veritas*," 613-34.
[62] J. Allen Cabaniss, "Agobard of Lyons," *Speculum* 26, no. 1 (1951): 59-61; Jacob Katz, *Exclusiveness and Tolerance: Studies in Jewish-Gentile Relations in Medieval and Modern Times* (London: Oxford University Press, 1961), 41-2; Rebecca Moore, *Jews and Christians in the Life and Thought of Hugh of St. Victor*, South Florida Studies in the History of Judaism 138, ed. Jacob Neusner, et al. (Atlanta: Scholars Press, 1998), 67-8; Elukin, *Living Together, Living Apart*, 46-7; Peter Schäfer, "Agobard's and Amulo's *Toledot Yeshu*," in *Toledot Yeshu ("The Life Story of Jesus") Revisited: A Princeton Conference*, ed. Peter Schäfer, Michael Meerson, and Yaacov Deutsch (Tübingen: Mohr Siebeck, 2011), 42-3.
[63] See Katz, *Exclusiveness and Tolerance*, especially 24-47.

Empire that, beyond denying Jesus' messiahship, they openly spread rumors (and recited every time they prayed)[64] that Mary had not been impregnated by the Holy Spirit, given birth to the son of God, Jesus, and raised him with his divinely elected foster father, Joseph, but that she had been "defiled," by an "impious man ... whom they [Jews] call Pandera," and had thus conceived Jesus.[65] Plainly put, this version of *Toledot Yeshu* suggests that Mary had been raped by a man who was not her fiancé/husband Joseph,[66] but an impious man named Pandera in a manner that undermined the doctrines of Virgin Birth and Incarnation.[67]

---

[64] Meerson and Schäfer, introduction to *Toledot Yeshu*, 47.

[65] "Confitentes eum esse impium et filium impii, id est, nescio cujus ethnici, quem nominant Pandera: a quo dicunt matrem Domini adulteratam, et inde eum in quem nos credimus, natum": Amulo Lugdunensis, *Liber Contra Judaeos*, in *Patrologia Latina*, 116:169D (Ateliers Catholiques: Paris, 1844-55).

[66] Contra Peter Schäfer, "Jesus' Origin, Birth, and Childhood according to the *Toledot Yeshu* and the Talmud," in *Judaea-Palaestina, Babylon and Rome: Jews in Antiquity*, ed. Benjamin Isaac and Yuval Shahar (Tübingen: Mohr Siebeck, 2012), 142; idem, "Agobard's and Amulo's Toledot Yeshu," in Schäfer, Meerson, and Deutsch, *Toledot Yeshu Revisited*, 27-48; and idem, Meerson and Schäfer, introduction to *Toledot Yeshu*, 9, who asserts that Amulo's text reads that Jews blasphemed Jesus by claiming that he was "impious and the son of an impious, namely, [someone] of uncertain origin (ethnici), whom they call Pandera: with whom (a quo) they say the mother of our Lord committed adultery (adulteratam) ..." Schäfer's interpretation of "a quo ... adulteratam" is questionable in that it presents Mary as an active party to adultery when the Latin of Amulo's account suggests she was a passive recipient of action—in this case, the victim of defilement. Pandera's active role and Mary's passivity are suggested through the ablative prepositional phrase "by whom" (*a quo*), followed by the accusative form of "mother" (*matrem*), indicating that action was done *to* mother Mary rather than *with* her. *Matrem* agrees in case, number, and gender with the perfect passive participle of "defile" (*adulteratam*), thus conveying that mother Mary had been the recipient of defilement—i.e., rape—by Pandera.

[67] See Natalie E. Latteri, "Playing the Whore: Illicit Union and the Biblical Typology of Promiscuity in the *Toledot Yeshu* Tradition," *Shofar* 33:2 (2015): 90-2.

As incendiary as this rhetoric might appear, the existence of some form of written Ashkenazic *Toledot Yeshu* is verified by Jewish sources, albeit significantly later. In the twelfth-century, Rabbi Ephraim of Bonn (1132-1200) mentioned a text similarly entitled *Tolada de Yeshu*.[68] Beyond this reference, Jewish anti-Christian polemic akin to that expressed by Celsus, Tertullian, and that found in the Babylonian Talmud, which would be incorporated into many versions of *Toledot Yeshu*, are also present in the multiple epithets for Jesus, common in Northern European Jewish texts.[69] These include insults that Jesus was the son of *ha-zonah*, "the whore," a *mamzer u-ven niddah*, "bastard son of a menstruating woman," or the combined *mamzer ben ha-niddah ha-zonah*, "bastard son of the menstruant whore."[70]

Amulo's claim that his neighboring Jews recited anti-Christian slander as part of their prayers may also have some merit. In the thirteenth-century Ashkenazic liturgy for Yom Kippur, the Day of Atonement, Israel was directed to sing to the Lord in affirmation of their Covenant with God while denouncing Mary as a promiscuous woman and Jesus as a bastard in the closing prayer: "The nations call 'Your Holiness' [i.e., Israel] to a son of whoredom [Jesus]; Your chosen ones despise the one conceived by the whore [Mary]."[71] The blending of a Jewish declaration of faith and penance found in this prayer is

---

[68] Meerson and Schäfer, introduction to *Toledot Yeshu*, 10.
[69] Anna Sapir Abulafia, "Invectives against Christianity in the Hebrew Chronicles of the First Crusade," in *Crusades and Settlement: Papers Read at the First Conference of the Society for the Study of Crusades and the Latin East and Presented to R. C. Smail*, ed. Peter W. Edbury (Cardiff, UK: University College Cardiff, 1985), 67; John G. Gager and Mika Ahuvia, "Some Notes on Jesus and his Parents: From the New Testament Gospels to the Toledot Yeshu," in *Envisioning Judaism: Studies in Honor of Peter Schäfer on the Occasion of his Seventieth Birthday*, vol. 2, ed. Ra'anan S. Boustan, et al. (Tübingen: Mohr Siebeck, 2013), 2:1009.
[70] Shlomo Eidelberg, *The Jews and the Crusaders: The Hebrew Chronicles of the First and Second Crusades* (Wisconsin: University of Wisconsin Press, 1977), 16, 144n10.; Limor, "Mary and the Jews," 58; Evyatar Marienberg, "Jews, Jesus, and Menstrual Blood," *De Gruyter Open* 14 (2016): 7.
[71] "Old Version of *Aleinu Le-Shabbe'ah*," quoted in Marienberg, "Jews, Jesus, and Menstrual Blood," 7.

further suggested in Ashkenazic Inquisitorial records. These show that, by the mid-fourteenth century at least, apostates who wished to revert to Judaism and incite Christians to kill them so that they might die as holy martyrs recited formulaic renunciations of Jesus as "an accursed bastard" and Mary as "the greatest of whores."[72]

As is the case with the second- and third-hand accounts mentioned above, parts of Amulo's account regarding the beliefs and practices of his Jewish neighbors can be corroborated. There was, in fact, a medieval Ashkenazic *Toledot Yeshu* tradition that included information about Jesus' conception, and some of the slanderous language associated with it was recited by Jews as part of religious ceremonies. But what of the details that Amulo mentioned that differ from Celsus, Tertullian, and the Babylonian Talmud? In those earlier accounts, and in many of the medieval epithets used to describe her, Mary was depicted as a promiscuous woman who consented to an illicit affair with a Roman soldier and conceived Jesus. In Amulo's version, by contrast, Mary was defiled by an impious man of uncertain religio-ethnic origin.

Unfortunately, we do not have an extant recension of *Toledot Yeshu* that mentions Jesus' conception until the fifteenth century, and the manuscripts of it and related versions date primarily from the seventeenth through nineteenth centuries.[73] Bearing this caveat in mind, each of the Ashkenazic accounts that we do have include the idea that Mary was a non-consensual party in Jesus' conception, as had Amulo. But the later *Toledot Yeshu* also include some notable variations and additions to Amulo's account. In them, Amulo's impious man of unknown religio-ethnic origin is identified as a wicked Jew; not only did he rape Mary, but he did so while she was menstruating. These later accounts reflect the development of Jewish critiques of the Virgin Birth and Incarnation in Northern Europe as well as mounting self-criticism regarding overfamiliarity with Christians and assimilation to Christian society. They also provide a revenge fantasy condoning

---

[72] Meerson and Schäfer, introduction to *Toledot Yeshu*, 15.
[73] See Meerson and Schäfer, introduction to *Toledot Yeshu*, 14-18, 50-1, 54.

violence in a manner that is not so dissimilar from that found in contemporary Christian apocrypha.

In the earliest account of Jesus' conception in Ashkenazic *Toledot Yeshu*, the reader is presented with a fuller narrative and Mary plays a far more substantive role than in Amulo's account. The tale begins with a depiction of Jesus' conception: Mary was a descendant of Israel and her fiancé, Yohanan, was of royal Davidic lineage. Yohanan was a good Jew, both God-fearing and well versed in Scripture. And one Sabbath's eve while he was away—presumably at Temple—a "good-looking"[74] neighbor named Yosef ben Pandera passed by Mary's house. In a drunken state, this good-looking Yosef went inside and began to behave as if he were her fiancé. Mary "thought in her heart that he was her fiancé Yohanan"[75] but, even so, when he began hugging and kissing her, she hid her face in shame and protested, saying, "Do not touch me, for I am menstruating."[76] Yosef "was not alarmed and did not pay attention to her words. He lay with her, and she conceived from him."[77]

When Yohanan returned in the middle of the night and sought Mary—presumably once Pandera had fled the scene—she asked him about his uncustomary behavior of (1) engaging in sexual activity twice in one night and (2) engaging in sexual activity while she was menstruating. In frustration, Yohanan left and told his rabbi what had happened. Shortly after discovering Mary's pregnancy and suspecting Pandera to be the father, Mary's fiancé Yohanan fled to Babylonia in shame, leaving Mary to bear and raise Jesus, seemingly alone and evidently without manners. For young Jesus had behaved disrespectfully to his teachers—much like the Jesus of the *Infancy Gospel of Thomas*—by asking difficult questions and showing his own mental superiority. As a result, one of the rabbis declared he

---

[74] Strasbourg, Bibliothèque Universitaire et Régionale, MS 3974, f. 170a, lines 4-5, in Meerson and Schäfer, vol. 2 of *Toledot Yeshu*, 82; Meerson and Schäfer, vol. 1 of *Toledot Yeshu*, 167.
[75] Ibid, 168.
[76] Ibid, 168.
[77] Ibid, 168.

was a "bastard," and another that he was a "bastard and the son of a menstruating woman"[78]—two epithets referencing Jesus' illegitimacy and inherently defiled status as an explanation for his wickedness.[79] Shortly thereafter, the rabbis paid Mary a visit and questioned her about Jesus' parentage. They determined that Mary was not liable for conceiving Jesus because Pandera's bad reputation preceded him and, surely, he was the culprit.[80]

In this account, the idea that Mary was a non-consensual victim of sexual assault is clear and her assailant's identity as a Jew is belied by the addition of a Hebrew name and patronymic, "Yosef ben."[81] But, in addition to these elements that appear to have built upon the ninth-century *Toledot Yeshu* that Amulo complained of, Mary rejected Yosef ben Pandera with verbal protests that referred to Jewish purity laws against copulating with a woman during her menses.

The Babylonian Talmud and response literature indicate that women often claimed to be menstruating when they were not to avoid unwanted advances. It was commonly believed that even a wicked man would refrain from raping a woman if he thought she was menstruating because she was like impure meat and the penalty for copulating with her during menstruating stipulated death by

---

[78] Ibid, 169.
[79] See Meerson and Schäfer, introduction to *Toledot Yeshu*, 46-9.
[80] Strasbourg, Bibliothèque Universitaire et Régionale, MS 3974, f. 170b, line 28, in Meerson and Schäfer, vol. 2 of *Toledot Yeshu*, 84; Meerson and Schäfer, vol. 1 of *Toledot Yeshu*, 170. Many scholars have noted that the story of Jesus as an arrogant yeshivah pupil, rabbinic name-calling of the youth as bastard son of a menstruant, and the questioning of the youth's mother about his parentage closely parallel *aggadah* from the Babylonian Talmud: see Marienberg, "Jews, Jesus, and Menstrual Blood," 3-4. Eli Yassif, "*Toledot Yeshu*: Folk-Narrative as Polemic and Self-Criticism," in Schäfer, Meerson, and Deutsh, *Toledot Yeshu Revisited*, 106-7, also relates this story to the *Toledot Ben Sira* and *The Arabic Gospel of the Infancy of the Savior*.
[81] William Horbury, "The Strasbourg Text of the *Toledot*," in Schäfer, Meerson, and Deutsh, *Toledot Yeshu Revisited*, 59, also notes that Pandera is not a Gentile in this recension; however, he thinks this marks a change from Amulo's account.

divine mandate.[82] In medieval Europe, this view was endorsed by the sages of the *Ḥasidei Ashkenaz,* or Pious of Ashkenaz. This group also promoted the belief that a child conceived of a menstruant would be unable to learn Torah properly or ever be counted among the pious but, instead, would be an idol worshipper whose moral nature was inherently flawed.[83] At the same time, Christians in medieval Europe were busy debating whether or not Mary menstruated. In part, this was owing to Aristotelian ecclesiastics' common association of menstruation with lust, of which the Church had proclaimed the Virgin void, but it was also owing to the fact that Jews had doubled down on their polemic against the Incarnation and claimed that God would never inhabit the filthy womb of a woman. In response, the Church came to the conclusion that Mary did not menstruate.[84] Thus the addition that she did in Ashkenazic *Toledot Yeshu* serves multiple polemical functions simultaneously.

In subsequent Askenazic *Toledot Yeshu,* the Jewish Pandera and the rape of a menstruating Mary would become more pronounced. In one version, the narrator indicates that Mary "screamed and cried out in a bitter voice and said, 'What are you doing now? I have just begun menstruating!'"[85] And, in the most popular version to circulate in Northern Europe[86] Yosef was not only Jewish but also a "pimp,

---

[82] See Israel M. Ta-Shma and Judith R. Baskin, "Niddah," in vol. 15 of *Encyclopaedia Judaica,* ed. Michael Barenbaum and Fred Skolnick, 2nd ed. (Detroit: Macmillan, 2007), 15:253-58; Yonah Lavery-Yisraeli, "Talmudic Descriptions of Menstruation," *Women in Judaism: A Multidisciplinary Journal* 13, no. 1 (2016): 9.

[83] Peter Schäfer, "The Ideal of Piety of the Ashkenazi Hasidim and Its Roots in Jewish Tradition," *Jewish History* 4, no. 2 (1990): 14; Cuffel, *Gendering Disgust,* 55-7, 104-05.

[84] Cuffel, *Gendering Disgust,* 71, 108-15, 120.

[85] New York, Library of the Jewish Theological Seminary of America, MS 2221, f. 39a, lines 17-18, in Meerson and Schäfer, vol. 2 of *Toledot Yeshu,* 97-8; Meerson and Schäfer, vol. 1 of *Toledot Yeshu,* 185-86.

[86] Meerson and Schäfer, introduction to *Toledot Yeshu,* 16-17.

an evil man, and [a] scoundrel ..."[87] But this version also includes other telling details that deserve consideration. In it, Yosef befriended Mary's fiancé Yohanan for the purposes of having his way with her. Mary warned her fiancé to avoid Pandera because she recognized him to be an evil man. But Yohanan protested, claiming that his own goodness might rub off and positively influence the scoundrel. Yohanan was wrong. Pandera got him so drunk that he passed out. And, as Yohanan slept, Pandera stole into Mary's house and pretended to be her exceedingly devout fiancé. He tricked her by turning out all the lights and reciting the *shema* (the Jewish declaration of faith, Dt. 6:4) with vigor. Even so, Mary rejected his advances because she was menstruating. To remedy the situation, Pandera lied and told her that a new *halakhah* had recently been determined that a man may copulate with his menstruating fiancée. Mary believed him and he had his way with her, once that night and then again, the next morning, thus conceiving Jesus.[88]

In each of these Ashkenazic *Toledot*, Mary conceives a bastard while menstruating. These two corrosive details mar Jesus *in utero* and lead to a disastrous severing of the Jewish community and the spawning of a new class of persecutors—Christians—in whose midst the Ashkenazic Jews who recounted these stories lived. In most cases, however, Mary is not presented so much as an adulterous or promiscuous woman but as a naïve victim who believed that her protests against sexual transgression might save her from defilement by any Jewish man who should have also been aware of the consequences of copulating with a woman during her menses, or as one who mistakenly believed that she could put her trust in a man known to be learned and pious but who she only later discovered had lied about both his identity

---

[87] Harvard University, Houghton Library, MS Heb. 57, f. 22a, line 2, in Meerson and Schäfer, vol. 2 of *Toledot Yeshu*, 213; Meerson and Schäfer, vol. 1 of *Toledot Yeshu*, 286.

[88] The entire conception narrative in this recension is found in Harvard University, Houghton Library, MS Heb. 57, f. 22a, line 1 through f. 22b, line 7, in Meerson and Schäfer, vol. 2 of *Toledot Yeshu*, 213-15; Meerson and Schäfer, vol. 1 of *Toledot Yeshu*, 285-87.

and the *halakhah* to serve his own purposes.⁸⁹ In these situations, Mary's victimization is not entirely dissimilar from that of medieval Ashkenazic Jews who, as early as the Carolingian era, protested what they perceived as lenient interpretations of *halakhah* by the rabbis. Especially devout members of the Ashkenazic community claimed that this leniency resulted in collective defilement that had incited God's wrath and, so, justified persecution against them.⁹⁰

When allusions to Mary's promiscuity are mentioned in Ashkenazic *Toledot*, they are typically faint. But statements of Yosef's good looks and repeated sexual coupling, once even in the light of day when confusion about who he was seems much less likely, suggests that Mary might not have completely balked at all of the impious Yosef's advances. In these cases, perhaps Mary was like the majority of Ashkenazic Jews who only initially—if ever—resisted *halakhic* leniency. Like her, they could appreciate some of the attractive benefits of not looking too closely into the legality of matters, however fleeting and ultimately disastrous it might be to do so.

Medieval Ashkenazim would also have identified with Mary's defilement in relation to the many medieval pogroms where Jews were forcibly converted. In rabbinic literature, forced converts are referred to as *anusim*.⁹¹ This term is also applied to the victims of rape, including the Mary of the Ashkenazic *Toledot Yeshu*.⁹² This

---

[89] Cf. Gager and Ahuvia, "Some Notes on Jesus and his Parents," 2:1009-13.
[90] See Ilia Rodov, "The Development of Medieval and Renaissance Sculptural Decoration in Ashkenazi Synagogues from Worms to the Cracow Area" (PhD dissertation, Hebrew University of Jerusalem, 2003), 31-3, 43.
[91] See Avraham Grossman, "The Roots of Kiddush ha-Shem in Early Ashkenaz" [Hebrew], in *The Sanctification of Life and Self-Sacrifice. A Collection of Articles in Memory of Aamir Yequtiel* [Hebrew], ed. I. Gafni and A. Ravitzky (Jerusalem: Zalman Shazar, 1992), 109, 111; Norman Roth, *Conversos, Inquisition, and the Expulsion of the Jews from Spain* (Madison: University of Wisconsin Press, 2002), 26; Eva Haverkamp, ed., *Hebräische Berichte über die Judenverfolgungen während des ersten Kreuzzugs* (Hannover: Hahnsche Buchhandlung, 2005): 48.
[92] The triliteral root סנא in Hebrew refers to rape or force. See "סנא" in Francis Brown, *A Hebrew and English Lexicon of the Old Testament*

connection between physical and spiritual defilement was concretized when Northern European Christians took Jewish women hostage in pogroms. Such occurrences became increasingly common after the 1096 pogroms accompanying the First Crusade. And when pogroms occurred, it was not uncommon for the Jewish community to suppose that the women had been both raped and forcibly converted. Having been thus doubly defiled, the women were perceptually transformed into different entities altogether—either non-Jews or prostitutes.[93] In seizing Jewish women, the Christian aggressors also emasculated the community's male population through the defilement of their mothers, sisters, wives, and daughters, and affirmed the subservience of the entire group under Christian rule.[94]

However the medieval Ashkenazim may have identified with the Mary of the *Toledot Yeshu* who had been lied to and assaulted, she, much more so than medieval Jewish women who had been compromised

---

(Oxford: Clarendon Press, 1978), 60. See New York, Library of the Jewish Theological Seminary of America, MS 2221, f. 39a, line 24, in Meerson and Schäfer, vol. 2 of *Toledot Yeshu*, 98.

[93] See the discussion of Rashi's interpretation of Mishnah *Ketubbot* 2:9 in Rachel Furst, "Captivity, Conversion, and Communal Identity: Sexual Angst and Religious Crisis in Frankfurt, 1241," *Jewish History* 22, nos. 1/2 (2008): 192. Rashi, for instance, promoted the idea that wives who had been seized in pogroms and forcibly converted were probably raped and, because they could subsequently corrupt those around them by virtue of their defiled status, need not necessarily be accepted as wives again by their husbands should they return to Judaism and their community.

[94] Furst, "Captivity, Conversion, and Communal Identity," 199. The thirteenth-century Rabbi Yitzhak ben Moshe went a step further by presuming that women who had been captured would use any means at their disposal to save their lives—not only succumbing to rape (as opposed to committing suicide and dying in *kiddush ha-Shem*), but also by using their bodies to seduce and ingratiate themselves to their tormentors. And R. Hai ben Sherira Gaon (d.1038) pronounced that a woman who had apostatized but who later repented and returned to the community was not a "Jew" in the same way that men who had once belonged to the community but who had willingly apostatized were considered by Rashi to have retained their inherent Jewishness; rather, such a woman became "like a harlot."

through rape or forced conversion, could not be counted as part of the Jewish community. For it was through the fruit of her womb that Israel had been severed in two. To prove that they could resist the temptation to become like and part of the dominant Christian culture Mary represented, the Jewish authors and propagators of *Toledot Yeshu* maligned her as a menstruant and/or whore to deny and deride the inviolate purity that Christians touted as a characteristic of her saintly status. They also defiled her literary persona in a manner that corresponded to the treatment of Jewish hostages and forced converts. In this way, the rape of Mary in Ashkenazic *Toledot Yeshu* may have functioned as an expression of revenge fantasy intended to harm Christians in ways comparable to the violence wielded by Christ against Jews in the apocrypha and, all the more so, the violence that Christ's followers continued to wield against Jews in reality.

Conclusion

Christian and Jewish stories about Jesus originating in the first centuries of the Common Era continued to develop throughout the Middle Ages. Their evolution provides clues to the socio-political contexts in which they were composed and promoted, especially as regards the shifting patterns of interfaith relations. For in each iteration, the stories provided doctrinal information, entertainment, and models of positive or negative behavior for their respective communities. The earliest Christian stories of Jesus found in the biblical Gospels and the *Infancy Gospel of James* reveal the insecurities and identity crises of communities so eager for acceptance by Jews and pagans alike that they presented Jesus as a fulfillment of Jewish messianic prophecy and the extended Holy Family as a bridge between "Old" and "New" covenants, even while adopting motifs from Hellenistic mythology. Early pagan and Jewish stories, by contrast, reveal some of the initial derision these groups showed for the emergent Christian doctrines of the Incarnation and Virgin Birth when they maligned Mary as a promiscuous woman who had engaged in a liaison with a Roman soldier.

Circumstances and alliances often change, and ideologies along with them. As Christianity spread throughout the Roman Empire and, later, the Germanic Successor States, Christian identity increasingly became linked with the polemical identification of Jews as outsiders who threatened the moral and social fabric of society. Late antique and early medieval apocrypha and iconography based on the *Infancy Gospel of Thomas* reflect and likely affected this ideological shift by depicting coercive conversionary efforts that appear to promote the marginalization of Jews and the physical abuse of those who resisted Christianity.

This ideology gained traction in step with large-scale Jewish immigration into Northern Europe at the behest of Charlemagne. The protections and privileges that the monarch (and subsequent rulers) provided to the Jewish community, and the feelings local Christians harbored of being slighted as a result of these, suggest that xenophobia and jealousy contributed to the fervor of anti-Jewish literary abuses. Ashkenazic Jews attempting to maintain their own unique religio-ethnic identity amid pressures and temptations to assimilate and/or convert to the dominant culture and religion responded in kind by developing regionally specific *Toledot Yeshu* tradition. In these, Jewish storytellers directed doctrinal polemics and literary abuses toward Jesus' mother while also projecting their own experiences as persecuted minorities onto Mary. The combination reflects the use of rhetorical resistance to assimilation and/or conversion when few other options were available, as well as the shared milieu of Jews and Christians living in contact and conflict.

Beyond the Pale
Hasidism, Neo-Hasidism and Jewish-Christian Dialogue

ARIEL EVAN MAYSE[*]

Foundation Stones

Hasidism is a product of the Eastern European milieu in which it was born. As a movement of a spiritual renewal that emerged and took root in the small sub-Carpathian villages of Eastern Europe, Hasidism and its spiritual vision have profoundly shaped the course of Jewish modernity. Disdain for the religion of the other was the regnant sentiment in that region, shared equally by Polish Catholics, Ukrainian or Belarusian Orthodox, and Jews. Although the presence of divinity in all elements of the cosmos, from the physical world to ordinary conversations in the marketplace, may rightly be described as a fundament of Hasidic theology, the Hasidic masters were also

---

[*] Ariel Evan Mayse is an assistant professor of Religious Studies at Stanford University and the rabbi-in-residence of *Atiq: Jewish Maker Institute* (https://www.atiqmakers.org). Previously he served as the Director of Jewish Studies and Visiting Assistant Professor of Modern Jewish Thought at Hebrew College in Newton, Massachusetts, and as a research fellow at the Frankel Institute for Advanced Judaic Studies of the University of Michigan. He holds a Ph.D. in Jewish Studies from Harvard University and rabbinic ordination from Beit Midrash Har'el in Israel.

heir to a stridently xenophobic and anti-Christian thrust within the Kabbalistic tradition. But the Hasidim were not only inheritors of mystical ideas; they, like the medieval Kabbalists, had experienced the antagonism of Christians first-hand. This fearful attitude toward the outside world exerted increasing force as the nineteenth century wore on, with Hasidic communities fighting to erect barriers and stem the tide of modernization.

The Hasidic vision of Christianity, fraught as it was with tension, anxiety and antipathy, was a source of struggle and contention for twentieth-century theologians who looked to the teachings of Hasidism as font of spiritual renewal. For this reason, a few brief notes on perceptions of Christianity in earlier Jewish mystical texts—and especially Hasidism—are in order. But the lion's share of our time will be devoted to exploring the works of Martin Buber, Abraham Joshua Heschel, and Zalman Schachter-Shalomi. These writers and teachers sought to spark a spiritual renewal of contemporary Jewish life by drawing from the well of Hasidic devotion. Their theological projects, though quite different from one another, should be seen as distinct voices within a burgeoning movement that has come to be known as Neo-Hasidism.[1]

By "Neo-Hasidism," I mean that Buber, Heschel, and Schachter-Shalomi each sought to translate the teachings of Hasidism and its spiritual ethos for an audience of seekers and intellectuals beyond the confines of Hasidic society, while simultaneously allowing modern concerns and values to permeate and shape their recasting of Hasidic piety. It is therefore of note that all three of these neo-Hasidic leaders had formative experiences with Christian theology and maintained long-standing relationships with Christian clergy and theologians. These connections, which influenced their writings to no small degrees, reflects the fact that Buber, Heschel, and Schachter-Shalomi were deeply engaged with the questions of interfaith dialogue. In

---

[1] On the development of Neo-Hasidism and its contemporary flourishing, see *A New Hasidism: Roots* and *A New Hasidism Branches*, ed. Arthur Green and Ariel Evan Mayse (Philadelphia: The Jewish Publication Society, 2019).

this vein, the present essay will conclude with a few hopeful remarks regarding the relevance of the legacies of Hasidism and Neo-Hasidism for contemporary inter-religious engagement through our shared commitment to social, moral and spiritual justice.

Siblings of Spirit

The relationship between Jewish mysticism and Christianity is long, complicated, and rife with discord. This tension-ridden dynamic stretches back into the formative moments of late Antiquity, since the earliest strata of what became Jewish mysticism emerged from the shared cultural heritage that gave birth to rabbinic Judaism and early Christianity.[2] As Jews sought to disentangle themselves from Christians, many rabbinic Jews came to consider Christianity to be *'avodah zarah* – idolatry – with all the prohibitions and implications thereof.[3] Such sentiments were tempered in the medieval Christian world, but the deep sense sibling rivalry sustained mutual antipathy between the Christian majority and the Jewish minority and was easily visible in Jewish mystical literature.[4] And yet, while having

---

[2] See Gershom Scholem, *Jewish Gnosticism, Merkabah Mysticism, and Talmudic Tradition* (New York: Jewish Theological Seminary of America, 1965); Ithamar Gruenwald, *Apocalyptic Merkavah Mysticism* (Leiden: Brill, 1980); Peter Schäfer, *The Origins of Jewish Mysticism* (Tübingen: Mohr Siebeck, 2009); and Arthur Green, *Keter: The Crown of God in Early Jewish Mysticism* (Princeton: Princeton University Press, 1997).

[3] For a more complicated picture, see Daniel Boyarin, *Border Lines: The Partition of Judaeo-Christianity* (Philadelphia: University of Pennsylvania Press, 2004).

[4] See Tosafot to b. 'Avodah Zarah 2a; Menahem Me'iri's comments on b. 'Avodah Zarah 26a; *Shulhan 'Arukh, yoreh de'ah* 148:12. See Arthur Green, *A Guide to the Zohar* (Stanford, CA: Stanford University Press, 2003), 88-89. More broadly, see Israel Jacob Yuval, *Two Nations in Your Womb: Perceptions of Jews and Christians in Late Antiquity and the Middle Ages*, trans. Barbara Harshav and Jonathan Chipman (Berkeley and Los Angeles: University of California Press, 2006); Jeremy Cohen, *Living Letters of the Law: Ideas of the Jews in Medieval Christianity* (Berkeley and Los Angeles: University of California Press, 1999); David Novak, *The Image of the Non-*

no real intellectual contact with the content of Christian theological discourse, medieval Jewish mystics were nevertheless influenced by images of piety and cultural currents that saturated the world in which they lived.[5] Such inter-cultural exchange is more visible to the modern scholar than it was to the medieval Jewish—or Christian—readership. A few early detractors of the Kabbalah, however, perceived some of its doctrines as a kind of heretical Christian import.[6] To paraphrase an infamous quip about the *sefirot*—the ten inner divine emanations at the heart of Kabbalistic theology: "Ten gods? That's even worse than three!"[7]

Jew in Judaism: An Historical and Constructive Study of the Noahide Laws (Lewiston, NY: Edwin Mellon Press, 1983), and Alan Brill, *Judaism and Other Religions: Models of Understanding* (New York: Palgrave Macmillan, 2010).

[5] Yehuda Liebes, "The Messiah of the Zohar: On R. Simeon bar Yohai as a Messianic Figure," *Studies in the Zohar*, trans. Arnold Schwartz, Stephanie Nakache, Penina Peli (Albany: State University of New York Press, 1982): 1-84; Arthur Green, "*Shekhinah*, the Virgin Mary, and the Song of Songs: Reflections on a Kabbalistic Symbol in its Historical Context," *AJS Review* 26, no. 1 (2002): 1-52; See also Moshe Idel, *Ben: Sonship and Jewish Mysticism* (London and New York: Continuum, 2007); Elliot R. Wolfson, "The Tree That is All: Jewish-Christian Roots of a Kabbalistic Symbol in *Sefer ha-Bahir*," *The Journal of Jewish Thought and Philosophy* 3, no. 1 (1994): 31-76; David Shyovitz, *A Remembrance of His Wonders: Nature and the Supernatural in Medieval Ashkenaz* (Philadelphia: University of Pennsylvania Press, 2017); Jonatan M. Benarroch, "'Son of an Israelite Woman and an Egyptian Man'—Jesus as the Blasphemer (Lev 24: 10–23): An Anti-Gospel Polemic in the Zohar," *Harvard Theological Review* 110, no. 1 (2017): 100-124; idem, "God and His Son: Christian Affinities in the Shaping of the Sava and Yanuka Figures in the Zohar," *Jewish Quarterly Review* 107, no. 1 (2017): 38-65; Ellen D. Haskell, *Mystical Resistance: Uncovering the Zohar's Conversations with Christianity* (Oxford University Press, 2016); and Ruth Kara-Ivanov Kaniel, *Holiness and Transgression: Mothers of the Messiah in the Jewish Myth* (Academic Studies Press, 2017).

[6] Gershom Scholem, *Origins of the Kabbalah*, trans. R. J. Zwi Werblowsky (Philadelphia: Jewish Publication Society, 1987), 14-15, 238.

[7] See Alon Goshen-Gottstein, "The Triune and the Decaune God: Christianity and Kabbalah as Objects of Jewish Polemics," in *Religious*

Starting in a somewhat later period, there is a well-known cast of Christian figures stretching into modernity – thinkers like Giovani Pico dela Mirandola, Johannes Reuchlin, Johann Kemper, and perhaps Gottfried Wilhelm Leibniz – who were engaged with the secrets of the Kabbalah, which they perceived as a kind of hermetic knowledge or as a doctrine that revealed universal truths.[8] Many of these Christian Kabbalists delighted in discovering this "true" inner Judaism, hoping to use it as a bridge toward justifying Christianity and evangelizing among Jews.

The resonances of affinity and subtle cultural borrowing found in medieval Kabbalah and Christianity are a far cry from the theological and intellectual openness manifest in Maimonides' thinly-veiled references to Al-Farabi and his unabashed reverence for Aristotle. The term *kabbalah* means "tradition," and its proponents claimed to maintain a chain of transmission—even if largely imagined— hearkening back to Sinai.[9] Although Jewish mysticism has clearly been shaped by its confrontation with a variety of external intellectual currents, most Kabbalists have continued to project their self-understanding as inheritors of a sustained internal discourse rooted in

---

  Polemics in Context, ed. by T.L. Hettema and A. van der Kooij (Leiden: Brill, 2005): 165-197, esp. 189-192.

[8] See, for example, Joseph Dan, ed. *The Christian Kabbalah: Jewish Mystical Books and their Christian Interpreters* (Cambridge: Harvard College Library (1997); Allison Coudert, *The Impact of the Kabbalah in the Seventeenth Century: The Life and Thought of Francis Mercury van Helmont (1614-1698)* (Leiden: Brill, 1999); Elliot R. Wolfson, "Messianism in the Christian Kabbalah of Johann Kemper," *Millenarianism and Messianism in Early Modern European Culture*, ed. Matt Goldish, et al (Dordrecht, Boston and Kluwer: Archives internationales d'histoire des idées, 2001), 139-187; Matt Goldish, "Newton on Kabbalah," *The Books of Nature and Scripture: Recent Essays on Natural Philosophy, Theology and Biblical Criticism in the Netherlands of Spinoza's Time and the British Isles of Newton's Time*, ed. James E. Force and Richard H. Popkin (Dordrecht and Boston: Kluwer Academic, 1994), 89-103.

[9] See Gershom Scholem, "Revelation and Tradition as Religious Categories in Judaism," *The Messianic Idea in Judaism* (New York: Schocken Books, 1995), 282-303.

divine revelation. Moreover, there is an unmistakable polemical thrust in medieval Kabbalah. Strong anti-monastic currents, for example, hover just beneath the Zohar's celebration the direct link between the "heavenly marriage" (*hieros gamos*) and its earthly corollary and, by contrast, the Zohar's condemnation of the spiritual bareness that results from celibacy.[10]

Kabbalistic antipathy toward Christianity and Christians, echoed in theological dismissals by Maimonides and other medieval rationalists, extends farther than doctrinal disputation or polemic.[11] The discourse of Jewish mysticism is in many respects rooted in a discourse of power, providing an internal Jewish answer to accusations of a shattered covenant and Christian supersessionism.[12] There is a deep and readily-apparent strain of essentialist xenophobia in Kabbalah.[13] This doctrine is found in pre-Kabbalistic works like the Rabbi Yehudah ha-Levi's *Kuzari*, continuing in an intensified form in the Zohar and the works of other Andalusian mystics.[14] The vision of the Jewish soul as inherently (even ontologically) distinct from those of all other human beings is particularly visible throughout the writings of Rabbi Yehudah Leib of Prague (better known as the MaHaRaL),

---

[10] See Arthur Green, "Intradivine Romance: The Song of Songs in the Zohar" *Scrolls of Love: Ruth and the Song of Songs*, ed. Peter S. Hawkins and Lesleigh Cushing Stahlberg (New York: Fordham University Press, 2006), 214-227.

[11] See David Novak, "Maimonides' Treatment of Christianity and its Normative Implications," *Jewish Theology and World Religions*, ed. Alon Goshen-Gottstein and Eugene Korn (Oxford: Littman Library of Jewish Civilization, 2012), 217-233; Daniel J. Lasker, "Tradition and Innovation in Maimonides' Attitude Toward Other Religions," Maimonides after 800 Years, ed. Jay M. Harris (Cambridge: Harvard University Center for Jewish Studies, 2007), 167-182.

[12] See, for example, Jonathan Garb, *Manifestations of Power in Jewish Mysticism* (Jerusalem: Magnes Press, 2005); and Hartley Lachter, *Kabbalistic Revolution: Reimagining Judaism in Medieval Spain* (New Brunswick: Rutgers University Press, 2014).

[13] See Elliot R. Wolfson, *Venturing Beyond: Law and Morality in Kabbalistic Mysticism* (Oxford and New York: Oxford University Press, 2006), 17-185.

[14] See Harry Austryn Wolfson, "Hallevi and Maimonides on Prophecy," *The Jewish Quarterly Review* 3, no.4 (1942): 353-370.

whose work exerted significant impact upon Hasidic thought. Some later thinkers, such as the late nineteenth-century Italian rabbi and Kabbalist Elia Benamozegh (1822-1900), sought to purge Jewish mysticism of this legacy.[15] But this essentialist xenophobia runs quite deep, and continues to exert its force upon Jewish life into the present.

Hasidism and Christianity

The mystical path of Hasidism emerged at the cross-roads of modernity, growing forth from the teachings of R. Israel ben Eliezer (d. 1760) of Mezhbizh.[16] This enigmatic figure, better known as the Ba'al Shem Tov, lived in Podolia (modern Ukraine) near the Carpathian Mountains. We know very little about his life that does not come from internal Hasidic sources, but legends tell of his humble beginnings followed by a period of prolonged solitude. In the 1730s the Ba'al Shem Tov began to share a new type to religious life that foregrounded the values of joy and ecstatic prayer. His theology and approach to worship eventually crystallized into Hasidism, one of the most important and successful Jewish movements of modernity.

Scholars have noted the similarity between the Ba'al Shem Tov's emphasis on religious ecstasy and the devotional attitudes of some Christian mystics living in this same region. The claim that the Ba'al Shem Tov may have been influenced by their religious ethos, vehemently rejected by Gershom Scholem, has recently been reconsidered a variety of scholars interested in examining Hasidism

---

[15] See Clémence Boulouque, "Elia Benamozegh (1823-1900): Kabbalah, Tradition and the Challenges of Interfaith Encounters", Ph. D. Dissertation, New York University, 2014.

[16] For two very different interpretations of this figure, see Moshe Rosman, *Founder of Hasidism: A Quest for the Historical Baal Shem Tov*, 2nd revised edition (Oxford and Portland: Littman Library of Jewish Civilization, 2013); and Immanuel Etkes, *The Besht: Magician, Mystic, and Leader*, trans. Saadya Sternberg (Waltham: Brandeis University Press, 2005).

as part of its Eastern European cultural milieu.[17] And, stepping away from question of direct historical influence, I should add that the noted scholar Rivka Schatz-Uffenheimer interpreted early Hasidism as a contemplative type of mysticism parallel to Christian Quietism.[18] Her thesis has been challenged in recent years, but the affinity she draws between Hasidic devotion and Christian mysticism remains an interesting case study of suggestive resonances between the spiritual teachings of distinct religious communities.

Taking up this question from a different angle, Shaul Magid has recently suggested a rather provocative thesis regarding the relationship between Hasidism and Christianity.[19] The medieval Jewish mystics who lived in close dialogue with Christianity and were thus forced to define themselves as separate with bitter polemics, but, argues Magid, Hasidism emerged outside the "glance" of Christianity and was therefore fearless of any affinity. This situation was quite different than, say, the intellectual project Moses Mendelssohn, another key

---

[17] See Torsten Ysander, *Studien zum Bceštschen Hasidismus in seiner Religionsgeschichtlichen Sonderart* (Uppsala: 1933); Yaffa Eliach, "The Russian Dissenting Sects and Their Influence on Israel Baal Shem Tov, Founder of Hasidism," *Proceedings of the American Academy for Jewish Research* 36 (1968): 57-83. For Scholem's rejection of her thesis, see Gershom Scholem, "The Neutralization of the Messianic Element in Early Hasidism," *The Messianic Idea in Judaism* (New York: Schocken Books, 1995), p. 362 n. 37. See Igor Tourov, "Hasidism and Christianity of the Eastern Territory of the Polish- Lithuanian Commonwealth: Possible of [sic] Contacts and Mutual Influences," *Kabbalah* 10 (2004): 73-105; Moshe Idel, "R. Israel Ba'al Shem Tov 'in the State of Walachia': Widening the Besht's Cultural Panorama," *Holy Dissent: Jewish and Christian Mystics in Eastern Europe*, ed. Glenn Dynner (Detroit: Wayne State University Press, 2011), 69-103.

[18] Rivka Schatz-Uffenheimer, *Hasidism as Mysticism: Quietistic Elements in Eighteenth Century Hasidic Thought*, trans. Jonathan Chipman (Princeton and Jerusalem: Princeton University Press and Magnes Press, 1993), esp. 65-69, 184-188, 111-143, 185-186, 190-192, 204-214.

[19] Shaul Magid, *Hasidism Incarnate: Hasidism, Christianity, and the Construction of Modern Judaism* (Stanford: Stanford University Press, 2015).

eighteenth-century figure whose writings included the defense of Jewish practices, exegesis, and so forth, against the incendiary criticism of Christian theologians like Immanuel Kant. Hasidic thinkers were surrounded by Christianity but were never forced to explain or justify their differences, internally or externally. This bitter distance and mutual distrust prevented any meaningful dialogue, but for this reason, Hasidism was free to develop notions that might elsewhere have been perceived as drifting toward Christian ideology.

The founders of Hasidism lived and taught in an intellectual framework where medieval and even pre-medieval certainties remained untouched by the critical challenge of nascent modernity. Any affinities aside, it is unsurprising that the literature of Hasidism is filled with a kind of anti-Christian legacy. This posture reflects centuries of persecution, of blood libels, of pogroms. Christianity—and it is hard to know if they made any distinctions between its various forms—was the religion of those who surrounded and oppressed the communities that gave birth to Hasidism.[20] The teachings of its masters, like the Kabbalistic theology to which they were heir, was dominated by a kind of ethno-centrism in which "Israel" and "humanity" are constantly identified.[21]

Hasidism has preserved very few explicit texts about Christianity. Rarely is the subject mentioned in sermons or homilies, which speak of "the nations of the world" (*umot ha-'olam*) or "non-Jews" (*goyyim*) but rarely of Christians. This is unsurprising, given the heavy hand of governmental (but Christian-based) censorship, but it also sets the early Hasidim apart from their medieval forebears for whom Christian and Islamic claims of supersession presented towering intellectual

---

[20] Cf. David Biale, *Eros and the Jews: From Biblical Israel to Contemporary America* (Berkeley and Los Angeles: University of California Press, 1997), 121-148. And for a different perspective, see Menachem Kallus, "Early Hasidic Ecumenism Up to the Mid-19th Century," *Chosenness and Ecumenism*, ed. Alon Goshen-Gottstein (forthcoming).

[21] This enfolding of humanity into Israel (and the more-than-occasional exclusion of non-Jews) is deeply rooted in the conceptions of power noted above.

challenges.²² Most Hasidic references to Christianity come in the form of villainous clergy in Hasidic hagiography.

Of course, thinly-veiled theological rancor undergirds these hagiographical works as well. One of these is a noteworthy tale included in the early compendium called "In Praise of the Ba'al Shem Tov" (*Shivhei ha-BeSHT*, Kopost 1814/1815), Hasidism's earliest sacred history of its own founders. This story tells of the departed spirit of Shabbatei Tsevi, the infamous heretic and false messiah, coming to the Baal Shem Tov in order to ask the Hasidic master to raise him out of purgatory and deliver him to heaven. The Ba'al Shem Tov tries to help him accomplish this task, acknowledging that a spark of divinity inheres even in fallen spirit of Shabbatai Tsevi. But the attempt collapses, and Shabbatai Tsevi plummets down into the pits of Hell until he reaches the lowest rung occupied by none other than Jesus himself.²³ We, as modern readers, may actually see a thread of commonality linking Christianity, Sabbateanism and Hasidism as three movements of religious renewal. Such a link was not unknown to the Neo-Hasidic thinkers to whom we shall turn shortly. But surely that could not have been understood or intuited by the author of this nineteenth-century text, a polemic comparing a recent apostate with the ultimate failed messiah whose image is seared into the Jewish imagination.

Slightly more temperate visions of the religious other have been preserved in Hasidic literature. Teachings in early Hasidic works seem to suggest, on one hand, that the boundaries of holiness are not determined by that which is purely Jewish. "The songs (*lieder*) of the

---

22   Mark R. Cohen, *Under Crescent and Cross: The Jews in the Middle Ages* (Princeton: Princeton University Press, 2008).

23   *In Praise of the Baal Shem Tov [Shivhei ha-Besht]: The Earliest Collection of Legends about the Founder of Hasidism*, trans. Dan Ben-Amos and Jerome R. Mintz (Northvale: Jason Aronson, Inc. 1993), no. 66, 86-87. Cf. ibid, no. 41, 54-58; no. 44, 59. See also Yehuda Liebes, "Hadashot le-'Inyan ha-BeSHT ve-Shabbatai Tsevi," *Sod ha-Emunah ha-Shabta'it* (Jerusalem: Mossad Bialik, 1995), 262-263; Paweł Maciejko, *The Mixed Multitude: Jacob Frank and the Frankist Movement* (Philadelphia: University of Pennsylvania Press, 2011), 2; and Joseph Dan, The Hasidic Story, (Jerusalem: Keter 1975, 118-123).

gentile singers," claimed Rabbi Moshe Hayyim Efrayim of Sudilkov, "are filled with aspects of awe and love that have spread out from on high, reaching all the lower levels."[24] This vitality is to be uplifted by the Jews, who were cast into exile in order to accomplish this sacred task.[25] In a recent essay, Glenn Dynner has referred to this Hasidic notion of uplifting the sparks trapped in the Slavic Christian culture as "a miraculous extraction of the pure from the impure."[26] But, miracle as it may be, Hasidic songs have more than once taken peasant folk piety and turned it into Jewish worship.[27] Rabbi Nahman of Bratslav (1772-1811) taught that non-Jewish folk stories are filed with divine sparks. His own richly symbolic stories embody this point: they incorporate motifs and characters common to multi-cultural folklore throughout Eastern Europe, such as princesses, kings, giants, dwarves, and witches.

Hasidism transformed significantly in the nineteenth and twentieth centuries, turning inward as the confrontation with new worlds and intellectual trends intensified fears of the outside. Direct engagement with Christianity, even polemic, remained a rare exception.[28] Hasidic leaders became a part of the traditionalist bloc rejecting any concession toward modernity or customs smacked of imitating "the ways of the gentiles" – foremost among them, changing dress, language, or

---

[24] *Degel Mahaneh Efrayim* (Jerusalem: 2013), *va-yera*, 39.

[25] See *Me'or 'Eynayim* (Jerusalem: 2012), vol. 1, *noah*, 27-28: "This also is the meaning of "They were comingled with the nations and they learned their ways" (Ps. 106:35). How could King David possibly have said such a thing about Israel? He wanted rather to explain why Israel are among the nations – so that they may fashion learning and Torah out of the deeds they do and out of their own involvement with the non-Jews. Think about this." Cf. *Kedushat Levi*, ed. Michael Derbaremdiger (Monsey: 1995) vol. 1, *devarim*, 368-369.

[26] Glenn Dynner, "Hasidism and Habitat: Managing the Jewish-Christian Encounter in the Kingdom of Poland," *Holy Dissent: Jewish and Christian Mystics in Eastern Europe*, ed. Glenn Dynner (Detroit: Wayne State University Press, 2011), 123.

[27] See *Hasidism: A New History*, ed. David Biale, et al (Princeton: Princeton University Press, 2018), 215-216.

[28] Magid, *Hasidism Incarnate*, esp. 116-117, 124-136

names.[29] The Holocaust that destroyed the Jews of Eastern Europe dealt a particularly harsh blow to the Hasidim, who eschewed emigration and were slaughtered by the Nazi agents of death. This rupture, though cataclysmic, was not the end of Hasidism. No one could have predicted that how the transplanted communities and survivors would reconstitute themselves around charismatic leaders and, within a generation, recreate their institutions, produce large new families that mostly remained faithful, and widely extend their influence within world Jewry. Hasidism has again become a major force in contemporary Jewish life and politics. But the modern-day Hasidim are not the only heirs to the spiritual legacy of its founders and their disciples.

Neo-Hasidism

We may now turn our attentions to the works of three twentieth-century Neo-Hasidic figures. Philosophical or religious Neo-Hasidism, which may be distinguished from the literary Neo-Hasidism of figures like I.L Peretz,[30] is a twentieth-century movement rooted in the quest for creativity and renewal at the heart of Hasidic devotion. Neo-Hasidism sees in Hasidism a mighty river of religious inspiration that can be marshalled for modern Jews – and non-Jews – who live their lives outside of the traditional Hasidic communities. Sensing that Hasidism has, by and large, become less vital over the centuries, due in part to the emergence of dynastic succession and the attempt to batten down all hatches in the face of the storm winds of

---

[29] See Michael K. Silber, "The Emergence of Ultra-Orthodoxy: The Invention of a Tradition," *The Uses of Tradition: Jewish Continuity in the Modern Era*, ed. Jack Wertheimer (New York: Jewish Theological Seminary of America, 1992), 23–84.

[30] See Nicham Ross, *A Beloved-Despised Tradition: Modern Jewish Identity and neo-Hasidic Writing at the Beginning of the Twentieth Century* (Beer-Sheva: Ben-Gurion University of the Negev press, 2010) (Hebrew); idem, "Can Secular Spirituality be Religiously Inspired?: The Hasidic Legacy in the Eyes of the Skeptics," *AJS Review* 37, no. 1 (2013): 93-113;

modernity, Neo-Hasidic thinkers often look to the vital figures of the Hasidism's early years for religious inspiration.

Neo-Hasidism also contends with a twofold disappointment in the contemporary world. It is a surely response to the lack of spirituality or lack of intellectual and theological openness in modern of Judaism. But the spiritual movement of Neo-Hasidism also reflects a lack of confidence in the secular world and the ideals of progress and modernization, which do not provide sufficient answers to questions of religion and existence that interest seekers drawn to neo-Hasidism. This ironic "disenchantment" with the ideas of human self-sufficiency and technological development is all the more unbearable for those of us who live after the Holocaust.

The works of Martin Buber, Abraham Joshua Heschel and Zalman Schachter Shalomi are suffused with the ethos of Hasidism, which they selectively translated and creatively reinterpreted in a contemporary key. All three saw Hasidism as embodying a particular devotional spirit, but they also understood the Hasidic quest for the Divine as representing a universal human longing for transcendence and uplift. Preserving medieval and pre-medieval attitudes toward Christianity would have been unthinkable for these religious thinkers, just as it would have been totally unimaginable for an eighteenth- or nineteenth-century Hasidic master to openly celebrate the power of Christianity.[31] And yet, the approaches of Buber, Heschel, and Schachter-Shalomi to Christianity were complicated and fraught with tension.

Renewal in Dialogue: Martin Buber

Let us begin with Martin Buber (1878-1965), an outstanding philosopher and theologian whose writings had a vast influence

---

[31] Regarding Neo-Hasidsm, interreligious dialogue, and the legacy of Jewish mysticism, see Or N. Rose, "Hasidism and the Religious Other: A Textual Exploration and Theological Response," *A New Hasidism Branches*, ed. Arthur Green and Ariel Evan Mayse (Philadelphia: The Jewish Publication Society, 2019).

on modern intellectual life. This includes a significant number of prominent Christian theologians, many of whom were avid readers of Buber's work.[32] Many of Buber's literary sources of religious inspiration were Jewish, and he was particularly drawn to biblical and Hasidic texts. But he was also influenced by a number of significant Christian thinkers and philosophers, and their works may well have colored his reading of Hasidic homilies and stories.[33]

Scholars often divide Buber's life and career into two distinct periods, though, as we shall see, sustained engagement with Hasidism was central to both of them. The young Buber was drawn to the mystical teachings of different religious traditions. His 1909 book *Ecstatic Confessions* explores how spiritual thinkers across the globe have effusively described their outpourings of the soul, presenting many of them to the German readership for the first time.[34] Although this particular collection is filled with everything *but* Jewish thinking on this subject, in these same years Buber had taken up Hasidism as an example of vital, authentic Jewish mysticism. He was particularly interested in the power of Hasidic stories, which, in his retelling, often glorify devotion through presence in ordinary deeds together with tales of rapture and uplift.

This infatuation with ecstatic mysticism faded, however, in the aftermath of Europe's Great War. Though initially a supporter of the conflict, Buber responded to the nationalist fervor and the killing fields left in its wake by developing an ethically-oriented spiritual vision grounded in lived, concrete encounters with other human beings. Buber's love of Hasidism extended into this second "dialogical"

---

[32] By Maurice S. Friedman, *Martin Buber: The Life of Dialogue* (Chicago: University of Chicago Press, 1955), 319-333; Guy G. Stroumsa, "Presence, Not Gnosis: Buber as a Historian of Religion," *Martin Buber: A Contemporary Perspective*, ed. Paul Mendes-Flohr (Jerusalem: Syracuse University Press and the Israel Academy of Sciences and Humanities, 2002), 25-47.

[33] Rivka Horwitz, "Buber and Ebner: Intellectual Cross-Fortilization Between a Catholic and a Jew." *Judaism* 32, no. 2 (1983): 188-195

[34] Martin Buber, *Ecstatic Confessions*, ed. Paul Mendes-Flohr, trans. Esther Cameron (San Francisco: Harper & Row, Publishers, 1985).

phase of his career, and he remained captivated by Hasidic sources that emphasized the evocative – indeed, the revelatory – power of interpersonal engagement. Hasidic homilies and tales, argued Buber, offer living testament to the sacred encounter between human beings. Such dialogue and communion summoned up a kind of spiritual experience without forcing the individuals to abandon their individual identities or moral obligations. This philosophy is perhaps most famously visible in his *I and Thou* (1923), but Buber's writings on Hasidism—from this period on—extoll the ethical and communal elements of religious experience.

The many works he penned across some five decades demonstrate that Buber was deeply interested in mobilizing biblical Jewish sources to spark contemporary religious renewal. His writings also evince a sustained engagement with Christianity, and with the figure of Jesus and his teachings in particular. Shaul Magid has insightfully highlighted the parallel between Buber's portrayal of the Baal Shem Tov and Jesus as critics of ossified religion.[35] He suggests, quite correctly, that "Buber drew a link between Jesus and the Baal Shem Tov… viewing the latter as a recapitulation, and correction of the former, one who created the conditions for the final overcoming of 'religion' and the return to an unmediated revelatory I-Thou relationship…"[36] At times Buber presents Jesus in contrast to Hasidic or Jewish devotion, but, more often, the teachings of Jesus are framed in comparison to the vital spirit of the *paterfamilias* of Hasidism.

Buber's longstanding affection for the spiritual genius of Jesus was well-known. In his 1951 book *Two Types of Faith*, he writes:

> From my youth onwards I have found in Jesus my great brother. That Christianity has regarded and does regard him as God and Saviour has always appeared to me a fact of highest importance which, for his sake and my own, I must endeavor to understand…

---

[35] Magid, *Hasidism Incarnate*, 113-136.
[36] Magid, *Hasidism Incarnate*, 115.

I am more than ever certain that a great place belongs to him in Israel's history of faith and that this place cannot be described by any of the usual categories.[37]

This fascination and admiration for Jesus was, of course, contrasted by Buber's utter disdain for the theology of Paul, whom he accuses of having turned the living faith of Jesus into a calcified, dogmatic theology laden with doctrine and sacrament rather than pure, lived devotion. Buber saw later Christianity as surrounding the spiritual core of Jesus' religiosity with "a mixture of a thousand rites and dogmas."[38]

Disdain for this same hyper-legalism characterized Buber's vision of rabbinic Judaism as well, and he saw Hasidism and its inward turn as the corrective needed for such a *nomos*-centered religion. Hasidism continued a focus on intentional presence that characterizes the teachings of Jesus as well: a sacred, living spontaneity that Buber deemed "religiosity" rather than the calcified structures of "religion."[39] This includes the courageous open-heartedness necessary to love the fellowship of humanity, another point of connection between Hasidism and Christianity. Buber writes:

> Hasidism is one of the great movements of faith that shows directly that the human soul can live as a whole, united in itself in communication with the wholeness of being, and indeed not merely individual souls, but a multitude of souls bound into a community… The clear flame of human unity embraces all forces and ascends to the divine unity.
>
> The unification of the ethical and religious spheres as it has been accomplished in exemplary fashion in Hasidism, even if only in a short-lived flowering, brings forth what we, in our human world, call holiness. We can know holiness as a human quality hardly otherwise than through such unification. It is important to come to know it.[40]

---

[37] Martin Buber, *Two Types of Faith* (Syracuse: Syracuse University Press, 2003), 12-13.
[38] Martin Buber, "Renewal of Judaism, in *On Judaism*, ed. Nahum N. Glatzer (Schocken Books: New York, 1996), 47.
[39] Buber, *Two Types of Faith*, 77-79.
[40] Martin Buber, *Hasidism and Modern Man* (New York: Harper & Row, 1958), ed. and trans. Maurice Friedman, 256.

This vital loving *communitas* was presented in Buber's later stage as one of the key messages of Hasidism, a mystical spirituality that does not force one to relinquish his ethical obligations to fellow human beings.

This means that for Buber, the dialogical encounter—a devotional moment as well as a moral turn—may reach beyond the confines of a single community. *Ich und Du* also holds the seeds for inter-religious dialogue and confrontation. Buber's dear friend and close collaborator Franz Rosenzweig saw the fraught proximity of Christianity and Judaism as giving rise to a fierce, uncompromising judgement. Buber saw things in a less draconian mode, but he too stressed that comparison between faith traditions as well as dialogue between them must not entail the surrender of one's particularity.

Buber was keenly aware of the issues in conflating religious traditions or comparing their writings unduly. "Religions," he writes, "are mansions into which the spirit of man is fit in order that it might not break forth and burst open its world. Each of them has its origin in a particular revelation and its goal in the overcoming of all particularly. Each represents the university of its mystery in myth and rite and thus reserves it for those who live in it."[41] Comparison is doomed to failure if one seeks to juxtapose a natural, intuitive knowledge of one's own tradition with the perceived edifice of another. Dialogical encounter and the engaged acknowledgement of the other, however, brooks no such limitations.

Martin Buber's reading of Hasidism had a measured impact on Christian thought. Paul Tillich highlighted Buber's "I-Thou" relationship as a model for the encounter between Christianity with Judaism. Tillich also noted, with touching sincerity, that Buber's writings opened up the language and devotion of mysticism. With its rich and living mystical heritage, this mode of religiosity is far more accessible to members of the Catholic Church than liberal

---

[41] Martin Buber, "Christ, Hasidism, Gnosis," *The Origin and Meaning of Hasidism*, trans. Maurice Friedman (New York: Horizon Press, 1960), 242. See ibid, 252-253, for his remarks on the devotional vitality of Hasidism and its morality vis-à-vis the terrible forces of Gnosticism.

Protestants.⁴² Buber's recasting of Hasidism focuses on sanctifying the world, emphasizing agency and responsibility and thus offering a path for bringing the intensity of God's presence into life without compromising the social responsibility carried by the religious person in the modern world. Tillich writes:

> ... Buber's reinterpretation of Hasidism is extremely valuable. It shows the possibility of a mysticism which does not contradict but which intensifies prophetic religion... Man is responsible for the destiny of God insofar as God is in the world; man is called to reestablish the broken unity in himself and in the world. God waits for man; and the answer to man's action is divine grace... It is the consecration of the moment, it is the simple act which is demanded from a special individual in a special situation, it is the acting of the anonymous people, the children and the simple ones. Such acting, if it is done in consecration, prepares the coming of the Kingdom of God. It is a messianic action.⁴³

This passage represents a deceptively multi-layered text. We find a Protestant theologian translating, into the terms of liberal Christianity, the words of a Neo-Hasidic philosopher and scholar, whose writings reinterpret Hasidism – a spiritual ethos that is itself a vital reworking of medieval Kabbalistic theology. And Tillich's very astute claim that Hasidism demands that the human being accept responsibility for "the destiny of God" will bring us directly to our next Neo-Hasidic figure.

Answering the Great Call: Abraham Joshua Heschel

Abraham Joshua Heschel (1907-1972) was one of the leading theologians and philosophers of religion in twentieth-century America.⁴⁴ Heschel was raised in the heart of Hasidic Warsaw and

---

42 Paul Tillich, "Martin Buber and Christian Thought." *Commentary* 6 (1948): 515-521,
43 Ibid, 519-520.
44 See Edward K. Kaplan and Samuel H. Dresner, *Abraham Joshua Heschel: Prophetic Witness* (New Haven and London: Yale University Press, 1998);

descended from prominent Hasidic leaders on both sides of his family.⁴⁵ He left Hasidic society because of its intellectual blinders, but he remained deeply engaged with the devotional ethos and teachings of Hasidism throughout his life. Much of his career was devoted to fostering a revival of post-war life in the US, grounded in the spirit of Hasidism. Key to this was his understanding on God's search for mankind, and the reciprocal obligations of the human being.⁴⁶ Visible already in the poetry of his youth, Heschel's focus on this them intensified greatly in the years after the Holocaust. Heschel lost nearly all of his family to the Nazi death machine, and he witnessed his world – that of the Eastern European Jews – sent up in smoke of the crematoria.

Though Heschel's theological writings are saturated with Jewish sources,⁴⁷ his interests and influences stretched far beyond the boundaries of Jewish culture. At the University of Berlin, he was immersed in classical works of moral philosophy, German Idealism, and phenomenology.⁴⁸ Heschel served on the faculty for many years at Jewish seminaries, including the Hebrew Union College in Cincinnati and then at the Jewish Theological Seminary of New York, but he also taught at Union Theological Seminary. It was Reinhold Niebuhr's review of his 1951 book, *Man is Not Alone,* that raised Heschel to the national stage of theology and philosophy.⁴⁹

---

and Edward K. Kaplan, *Spiritual Radical: Abraham Joshua Heschel in America, 1940-1972* (New Haven and London: Yale University Press, 2007).

⁴⁵ See Arthur Green, "Abraham Joshua Heschel: Recasting Hasidism for Moderns," *Modern Judaism* 29, no. 1 (2009): 62-79.

⁴⁶ See Arthur Green, "God's Need for Man: A Unitive Approach to the Writings of Abraham Joshua Heschel," *Modern Judaism* 35, no. 3 (2015): 247-261.

⁴⁷ See Michael Marmur, *Abraham Joshua Heschel and the Sources of Wonder* (Toronto: University of Toronto Press, 2016), 176-177.

⁴⁸ Shai Held, *Abraham Joshua Heschel: The Call of Transcendence* (Bloomington, IN: Indiana University Press, 2013), 72-93, who situates Heschel in dialogue with neo-Orthodox theologian Karl Barth and liberal Paul Tillich.

⁴⁹ Kaplan, *Spiritual Radical,* 120-121.

Although the renewal of Judaism was, without a doubt, Heschel's central project, his abiding interest in the renewal of the Church is critical as well. Heschel was deeply invested in this regeneration, and he had great belief in the power of Christianity to reckon with its own complicated history and to formulate a new theological vision infused with a spirit of tolerance as well as spiritual depth. Key to this renewal, said Heschel, was what he called a "confrontation with Judaism out of which it emerged."[50] Having grown forth from the font of Judaism, modern Christians could not afford to cut themselves off from their biblical and Jewish roots. For Heschel, this courageous reckoning meant a renewed commitment to the Hebrew Bible—not simply as an "Old Testament" filled with allegorical references to the coming of Jesus, but as a key text for understanding early Christianity and as a vital, soulful document with ethical wisdom to offer twentieth-century Christians.

The Bible, taught Heschel, sets forth the most fundamental theological question: "What does God require of me." And, he argues, Scripture offers the only fitting answer to this call: "Here I am!"[51] Heschel also suggests that the Hebrew Bible reveals a basic spiritual tenet that is shared by Jews and Christians alike: God cares deeply about the affairs of humanity, and we are thus called to respond through compassion and courage.[52] This call penetrates through the boundaries that separate religions. "The task of Christian renewal," says Heschel "…is above all the renewal of man, and the renewal of man is the *renewal of reverence*."[53] The legacy of wonder is the root of his moral philosophy, demanding prophetic engagement in the moral fabric of the world, including outcries against iniquity and outrage. Claims of human-centered progress, said Heschel, were mute after

---

[50] Abraham Joshua Heschel, "The God of Israel and Christian Renewal," Moral Grandeur and Spiritual Audacity: Essays, ed. Susannah Heschel (New York: Farrar, Straus and Giroux, 1996), 272.
[51] Ibid, 274.
[52] Ibid, 276.
[53] Heschel, "The God of Israel and Christian Renewal," 275. Emphasis in the original.

Auschwitz, Hiroshima, and the atrocities of Vietnam. In the ashes of this hubris, attunement to God's *pathos* and to the divine word are essential to the survival of civilization and the project of humanity.

The presence of dialogue, for Heschel as for Buber, was critical to forging a path of renewal. Unlike his contemporary Rabbi Joseph B. Soloveitchik, Heschel believed in a common core of religious experience that transcends religious traditions and is therefore universally accessible.[54] This fundamental assumption about the nature of spiritual experience influenced approach to inter-religious dialogue:

> I believe that one of the achievements of this age will be the realization that in our age religious pluralism is the will of God, that the relationship between Judaism and Christianity will be one of mutual reverence, that without denying profound divergences, Jew and Christian will seek to help each other in understanding one's respective commitment and in deepening appreciation of what God means.[55]

Heschel was deeply committed to a specific project, to the renewal of Jewish life and theology in light of the moral and spiritual teachings of the Hebrew Bible. Together with his appreciation of religious experience across faith traditions, the vision of the *Tanakh* provided Heschel with a vocabulary for tackling the broader issue of God's place in the modern word. On more than one occasion Heschel described "Who is Man?" as the question that shatters all complacency.[56] In seeking to answer this moral, philosophical, and theological enigma, Heschel marshalled the full array of Jewish sources. But he recast them in a key that rendered them widely accessible and, moreover, which framed the Jewish sources as responding to enduring human questions that cut across all denominational borders. At the heart of

---

[54] Reuven Kimelman, "Rabbis Joseph B. Soloveitchik and Abraham Joshua Heschel on Jewish-Christian Relations," *Modern Judaism* 24, no. 3 (2004): 251-271.

[55] Heschel, "The God of Israel and Christian Renewal, 272.

[56] Abraham Joshua Heschel, *Who is Man?* (Stanford: Stanford University Press, 1965).

this quest for renewal, said Heschel, lay the prophetic tradition of the Hebrew Bible.

Given this biblical emphasis and Heschel's emphasis of the universality of the Hebrew Bible—an accent immediately visible in his written works and public addresses – should Heschel's active, and sometimes critical, involvement in *Nostra Aetate* be seen as an outgrowth of his reading of Hasidism? Buber's theory of dialogue, including the encounter between communities of faith, was closely intertwined with his own idiosyncratic interpretation of the religious traditions of Hasidism. Was it so for Heschel?

This is a particularly thorny question. Although the ethical voice of the Hasidic masters informed his readings of all Jewish texts, Heschel's engagement with inter-religious dialogue and Vatican II reflected his biblical theology. Unlike his Yiddish poetry or his rabbinic theology penned in Hebrew, Heschel's English writings are knowingly resonant with the language of Christian devotion that is rooted in the biblical tradition. Heschel's investment in Christian renewal and rapprochement must be linked to his involvement in issues of social concern, including his outspoken opposition to the Vietnam War, and his commitment to the struggle for civil rights and the plight of Soviet Jewry. Influenced by Buber, Karl Barth, and other twentieth-century theologians who took the biblical word very seriously, Heschel's commitment to these causes reflected his reading of the prophets and their divine *pathos* as re-read through the spiritual lens of Hasidism. It is no coincidence that the young Heschel wrote his doctoral dissertation on the phenomenology of the prophets while living in Berlin during Hitler's ascent to power. His expanded translation of this work took place as his involvement with the push for Civil Rights, reflecting his concern for humanity as a universal value and spurring him to speak out and march on behalf of a disenfranchised minority.

Heschel's participation in all of these social causes should be seen as a response to the divine question that pulses at the heart of the Hebrew Bible: "Where is man?" How are we to respond to this call? What sort of life does God demand that we lead, asked Heschel by way of the prophets? A life of joy and exaltation, of presence and renewal, but also a life that is filled with care, compassion and concern for others. "A religious man is a person who holds God and man in one thought at one time, at all times, who suffers in himself harm done to others, whose greatest passion is compassion, whose greatest strength is love and defiance of despair."[57] God is in need of our deeds. Love, says Heschel, opens the human heart and allows the spirit to reach beyond the confines of the ego, coming to encompass the Divine and fill the world with God's presence.

Aquarian Hasidism: Zalman Schachter-Shalomi

We turn now to the late Rabbi Zalman Schachter-Shalomi (1924-2014), the founder of the Jewish Renewal movement and an exceptionally creative and dynamic spiritual teacher.[58] Born in Poland but raised in Vienna, he came of age in a diverse Jewish environment. His family had connections to the Hasidic world, but, living in a major metropolitan center, the young Zalman was exposed to a wide variety of Jewish religious and cultural expressions. After passing through Belgium and France to escape the Nazis, Zalman's family moved to the United States in 1941. Studying in Brooklyn, he became close to the Lubavitch leadership, which recognized his brilliant intellect and charismatic talents. Reb Zalman's spiritual awakening eventually led him far beyond the Orthodox community altogether, but throughout the spiritual quest that was his life, Reb Zalman—as he is affectionately known—looked to Hasidic teachings for inspiration and recast them for a contemporary audience of seekers.

---

[57] Abraham Joshua Heschel, *Moral Grandeur and Spiritual Audacity: Essays*, ed. Susannah Heschel (New York: Farrar, Straus and Giroux, 1996), 289.
[58] See Zalman M. Schachter-Shalomi, *My Life in Jewish Renewal: A Memoir*, with Edward Hoffman (Lanham, MD: Rowman and Littlefield Publishers, Inc., 2012).

Reb Zalman's discovery of the spiritual riches of Catholicism was a particularly important milestone in his spiritual journey.[59] In the Catholic tradition, Reb Zalman found a vast library of spiritual treatises on prayer, devotion, and the mystical life. Few Jews outside of the tight-knit Hasidic community were talking about such matters in mid-century America. In addition to amplifying the spiritual skills he had found and studied in Habad, Reb Zalman was stirred by the encounter of such profound knowledge in another faith tradition. He was now well aware and increasingly appreciative of the spiritual disciplines of other religious communities. Reb Zalman's sense of the problematic strictures of Orthodoxy, particularly what he perceived as its intellectual myopia—especially in terms of other religious traditions—had led him to explore religious vistas. He became a student of the Protestant theologian and preacher Howard Thurman, who exposed him to other religious traditions, particularly the powerful piety of his own mystical African-American Christian faith. Thurman also taught him a great deal about spiritual leadership in community, in particular how religion could be taught in an experiential manner.[60]

Catholic monasticism and its focused, disciplined approach to the inner life in the context of a community held a particular appeal for Reb Zalman.[61] He spent time in Catholic monasteries in the late 1950s and '60s, like the Abbey of Our Lady of the Prairies, eventually becoming a close friend and correspondent of Thomas Merton,

---

[59] The first full treatment of this dimension of Schachter-Shalomi's thinking will be treated in Or N. Rose's forthcoming dissertation entitled "The Making of a Mystical Pluralist: Zalman Schachter-Shalomi's Interreligious Journey." See also Ariel Evan Mayse, "Renewal and Redemption: Spirituality, Law and Religious Praxis in the Writings of Rabbi Zalman Schachter-Shalomi," *The Journal of Religion* (forthcoming).

[60] See Edward K. Kaplan, "A Jewish Dialogue with Howard Thurman: Mysticism, Compassion, and Community," *CrossCurrents* 60 (2010): 515–525.

[61] See Or N. Rose, "Envisioning a *Jewish* Monastic Community: Zalman Schachter, Catholicism, and the B'nai Or Fellowship" (unpublished).

Leo Rudloff, and many others.⁶² Reb Zalman wrote a brief treatise outlining the contours of a Jewish monastic order influenced by a combination of Hasidism and Christian monasticism.⁶³ Though the group never quite came to be in this form, it represented an effort to take the focused intentionality of Hasidism and transform it into a very different kind of modern monastic fellowship.

Such attempts to blend the essential wisdom of different faith traditions continued throughout Reb Zalman's life. He was criticized for being overly-syncretistic, incorporating language and practices from other faith traditions, and too little demanding of Jewish depth and knowledge. Reb Zalman's embrace of Aquarian religion and its vaunted New Age optimism remained a point of difference between he and other Neo-Hasidic thinkers like Arthur Green.⁶⁴ But Reb Zalman was far from casual about his engagement with other religious communities and their beliefs and practices. He was deeply concerned with the question of inter-religious dialogue—and its limitations. Reb Zalman described such conversations as requiring a fundamental posture of humility and an awareness that "acts of faith are not the result of facts."⁶⁵ Human beings have the capacity to bear witness, but we have nothing to gain by inflating the truth claims

---

62   Schachter-Shalomi, *My Life in Renewal*, 107-113, 115; Or N. Rose, "Reb Zalman, Neo-Hasidism, and Inter-Religious Engagement: Lessons from My Teacher," *Tikkun* 32, no. 4 (2017), 40-72.

63   Zalman Schachter-Shalomi, "Toward an "Order of B'nai Or": A Program for a Jewish Liturgical Brotherhood," *Judaism* 13.2 (1964): 185-197. Reb Zalman's vision for the community was influenced also by newfound Qumran documents and the Essenes.

64   See also Zalman Schachter-Shalomi, *Fragments of a Future Scroll: Hassidism for the Aquarian Age*, ed. Philip Mandelkorn and Stephen Gerstman (Germantown, PA: Leaves of Grass Press, 1975); and idem, *Paradigm Shift: From the Jewish Renewal Teachings of Reb Zalman Schachter-Shalomi* (Northvale, NJ: Jason Aronson, 1993).

65   Zalman Schachter-Shalomi, "Bases and Boundaries of Jewish, Christian, and Moslem Dialogue," in *Paradigm Shift: From the Jewish Renewal Teachings of Reb Zalman Schachter-Shalomi*, ed. Ellen Singer (Northvale, NJ: Jason Aronson, 1993), 21.

of one's own tradition or seeking to tear down those of others; such theological battles inhibit meaningful engagement.

The collapse of grand narratives, however, and the commitment awakening to a new era makes room for a different kind of multi-dimensional encounter. Reb Zalman advocated for what he called "the dialogue of the devout," which, in the post-modern world, can span across denominational and religious lines to encompass seekers of all faiths. This requires a robust and confident appreciation of difference: "Only by holding on to our shape and color do we form the mosaic in which we are God's tiles."[66]

Hasidic devotion and in particular, its approach to charismatic leadership, offer a point of connection for Jews and Christians. Though in later years Reb Zalman expressed frustration with Christianity's declarations of redemption through Jesus despite the painful brokenness of the world, he notes that the teachings about the *tsaddik* afford a plane of discussion. "Jews of mystical… Kabbalistic-Hasidic persuasion," says Reb Zalman, "seem to have a stronger theological warrant for dialogue. The *tzaddik* is God's possibility, for humanity in a physical body. The *tzaddik* is Torah, who decrees and God agrees."[67] The devotion of followers of Jesus has something very deep in common with the admiring love of the Hasidim for their *rebbe*.

A vision of God's ever-flowing and all-consuming love affords another point of connection for such conversations between Jews and Christians, as does the flexibility of their divine ontology – the Trinity vis-à-vis the *sefirot*. If such discussions do not descend into spats over theological truth, but rather serve to open engagement and mutual awareness, then these points of contact between the Jewish and Christian mystics may be fertile ground indeed. We should note that it is quite similar to Reb Zalman's with the Dalai Lama described

---

[66] Ibid, 31. Cf. Zalman Schachter-Shalomi "Jesus in Jewish-Christian-Moslem Dialogue," in *Paradigm Shift: From the Jewish Renewal Teachings of Reb Zalman Schachter-Shalomi*, ed. Ellen Singer (Northvale, NJ: Jason Aronson, 1993), 33-37

[67] https://havurahshirhadash.org/jesus-in-jewish-christian-moslem-dialogue/

by Roger Kamenetz in *The Jews in the Lotus*, albeit one in which the mutual appreciation will need to overcome centuries – millennia – of outright animosity.

In his short book *Foundations of the Fourth Turning of Hasidism*, published shortly before his death, Reb Zalman describes the need to cultivate a sense of "deep ecumenism." Drawing on the writings of Matthew Fox, Reb Zalman notes that:

> … as we explore the deep structures of our own traditions, revealing the basic functionality beneath the specific wrappings, we cannot ignore their similarity to those of every other religious and spiritual tradition on the planet…
>
> the Hasid must go beyond such surface knowledge, seeking the spirit beneath the external forms and teachings, undertaking the more intrepid explorations of "deep ecumenism," in which one learns about *oneself* through participatory engagement with another religion or tradition.
>
> Judaism can no longer afford to see itself as the only valid religious tradition, or even as the most important. For such a view is ultimately self-defeating and destructive to the ecological system of the planet which prefers diversity and depends on it for its own health. From this ecological perceptive, every religion is like a vital organ of the planet; and for the planet's sake, each must remain healthy, functioning well in concert with the others for the health of the greater body. Thus, Jews must be the best and healthiest Jews they can be, doing their part in the planetary eco-system; but they must also do it in a way that recognizes the contributions of other religions and supports their healthy functioning.[68]

Searching for such connections in the deepest structures of faith, experience, and ritual was a key element of Reb Zalman's recasting of Hasidism. His Neo-Hasidic project sought to penetrate to the core of religious meaning in Judaism, from theology to rituals, and thus allows for an appreciation of similar reservoirs of meaning in other

---

[68] Zalman Schachter-Shalomi and Netanel Miles-Yepez, *Foundations of the Fourth Turning of Hasidism: A Manifesto* (Boulder: Albion Andalus, 2014), 19-20.

faith traditions. There are multiple ways to attain such devotion, said Reb Zalman, all of which lead to the same Source. The survival of our planet and the continuation of civilization will rise or fall based on our ability to apprehend this truth and to live according to its wisdom.

Contemporary Moments, Future Directions

Jewish-Catholic dialogue has radically transformed in the decades following *Nostra Aetate*. This axial shift in Church policy has yielded many positive changes for the relationship between Jews and Catholics.[69] This openness has brought about new possibilities for deeper theological engagement although the question of inter-religious dialogue and the encounter between the two faith traditions is, of course, still fraught with complexity.[70] It is deeply gratifying to have come of age at such a moment in history, one in which the seeker may read across the boundaries of spiritual traditions in the quest for wisdom, insight and inspiration without compromising one's religious integrity.

The writings of figures like Francis X. Clooney model the power of a comparative theology in our day, a vision driven by intellectual honesty, spiritual openness, and academic rigor—all brought to bear in the quest to stand in the presence of the

---

[69] Some voices have claimed that a Third Vatican Council might move this even farther, perhaps including some of the more forthright positions in the original drafts of *Nostra Aetate* which confront the legacy of Catholic anti-Semitism more directly; see James Carroll, *Constantine's Sword: The Church and the Jews* (Boston and New York: Houghton Mifflin Company, 2001), 547-604; and Arthur Green, "The Sin of the Church," *Tikkun* 16, no. 3 (2001): 65-72.

[70] See Irving (Yitz) Greenberg, "Cloud of Smoke, Pillar of Fire: Judaism, Christianity and Modernity after the Holocaust," *Auschwitz: Beginning of a New Era?: Reflections on the Holocaust*, ed. Eva Fleischner (New York: Kav Publishing Company, 1977); and and idem, "Theology after the Shoah: The Transformation of the Core Paradigm," *Modern Judaism* 26, no. 3 (2006): 213–39.

One.[71] Without papering over the theological gulf that separates Jews and Christians, it is increasingly possible to share the collective wisdom of the human spirit and the yearning for the Divine. This moment in history also affords Jews and Christians an opportunity to work together, drawing upon their distinct theological legacies, to gather momentum in the fight for common good.[72] In this vein, rather than engaging in a kind of explicit theological dialogue—be it a quest for common ground or fruitful exploration of distinctions and tensions—this essay closes with an exploration of four issues of critical contemporary importance.

Jews and Christians will, of course, have rather different ways of understanding and articulating the theological dimension of the values that undergird the four issues. These distinct voices are sustained by our religious literatures, by our conceptions of God and the place of the Divine within the human realm. And yet, the fight for social, economic and ecological progress reflects Jewish values, Christian values, and deeper human values. Here, too, Heschel's wisdom and courage serve as a guidepost. In a 1965 lecture, he argued as follows:

> The supreme issue is today not the *halacha* for the Jews or the Church for the Christian—but the premise underlying both religions, namely, whether there is a *pathos*, a divine reality concerned with the destiny of man which mysteriously impinges upon history; the supreme issue is whether we are alive or dead to the challenge and the expectation of the living God. The crisis engulfs all of us. The misery and fear of alienation from God make Jew and Christian cry together.[73]

---

[71] See, for example, Francis X. Clooney, *Beyond Compare: St. Francis de Sales and Sri Vedanta Desika on Loving Surrender to God* (Washington, D.C.: Georgetown University Press, 2008); idem, *His Hiding Place is Darkness: A Hindu-Catholic Theopoetics of Divine Absence* (Stanford: Stanford University Press, 2014); and, most recently, idem, How to Do Comparative Theology (New York: Fordham University Press, 2018).

[72] Andrew V Ettin, and Ulrike Wiethaus, "Mysticism, Experience, and Pedagogy in Jewish-Christian Dialogue." *Studies in Christian-Jewish Relations* 4.1 (2009): 1-13.

[73] Abraham Joshua Heschel, "No Religion is an Island," *Moral Grandeur and Spiritual Audacity: Essays*, ed. Susannah Heschel (New York: Farrar, Straus and Giroux, 1996), 236

This is the ultimate question, a matter of supreme importance, which undergirds spiritual renewal in the modern era across faith traditions: Can religious people draw strength, together, from the wells of our tradition to combat the forces of hatred, indifference, cruelty? Heschel's voice gives us strength, calling us—as individuals of different faith communities yearning to repair this fractured world—to compassion, openheartedness, courage rooted in our vision of the divine.

For many involved in the project of Neo-Hasidism, such dialogue and shared striving is a critical element of our legacy and its future work. Infused with the dialogical and mystical sprit of Hasidism, Martin Buber also reflected on the ways in which Christians and Jews must work together. Despite the intractable differences that define respective faith communities, human beings may—and must— together pave the way for the kingdom of Heaven:

> What have you and we in common? If we take the question literary, a book and an expectation.
>
> To you the book is a forecourt; to us it is the sanctuary. But in this place we can dwell together, and together listen to the voice that speaks here. That means that we can work together to evoke the hurried speech of that voice; together we can redeem the imprisoned living word.
>
> Your expectation is directed toward a second coming, ours to a coming which has not been anticipated by a first... But we can wait for the advent of the One together, and there are movements when we may prepare the way before him together.[74]

Christianity and Judaism walk very different paths, and preserving such distinctions is crucial for our sense of integrity and authenticity. But Jews and Christians are also united in their commitment to sacred action, to summoning the divine Presence into the world through healing the cosmic fracture and easing the human suffering that is made obvious on a daily basis.

---

[74] Martin Buber "The Two Foci of the Jewish Soul," *Israel and the World: Essays in a Time of Crisis* (New York: Schocken Books, 1963), 39

Moral Audacity and Expanding the Boundaries of Holiness

The first of these critical issues is climate change and the looming environmental disaster that will surely come to pass if human greed and overconsumption continue unabated. Pope Francis's encyclical on ecology and climate change (*Laudato Si*) is a watershed moment, for it represents one of the most stirring descriptions of humanity's mandate to protect the world as nothing less than divine command. Rather than domination of the planet, Pope Francis urges members of the Church to approach the world with a sense of reverence, love, and responsibility, taking action to ensure that God's world is not destroyed through human apathy and carelessness.

The Hasidic vision of the world as suffused with the divine Presence should spur us to action to preserve its majesty and splendor.[75] These spiritual masters described every aspect of the cosmos as illuminated with God's sacred vitality, an ever-rushing life-force that animates all existence and brings the world into being anew in each and every moment. Such a world, one that pulses with vital divine energy and shimmers with God's majesty, is not meant to be dominated, to be stripped of its resources—to be fracked and sundered in an attempt to conjure up an endless stream of consumer goods.

The world is a dwelling place for the Divine, a stained-glass window composed of fragile apertures through which God's radiances shines. The command to preserve the world is also grounded in Hasidic teachings on God's *need* for human deeds, a concept that is rooted in the deepest ground of Hasidic theology. This message reminds contemporary seekers and religious individuals that we human beings have a grave responsibility as shepherds of this world, to uplift it and allow the sacred energy coursing through it to shine and shimmer with the infinite vitality.

---

[75] See the arguments put forward in David Mevorach Seidenberg, *Kabbalah and Ecology: God's Image in the More-Than-Human World* (New York: Cambridge University Press, 2015).

The second issue is that of a moral economy in which ethical and spiritual values are foregrounded high above fiscal bottom lines. This subject was treated in brief in *Laudato Si* and addressed more directly in the document titled "A Catholic Framework for Economic Life" (1996), a statement put out by U.S. Catholic Bishops. In that deeply moving document, we read: "All economic life should be shaped by moral principles. Economic choices and institutions must be judged by how they protect or undermine the life and dignity of the human person, support the family and serve the common good."[76] The issues in the modern economy that confront those fighting for progressive values from a religious perspective are legion: insufferable working conditions; unequal pay for women; terrible discrimination against people of color, ethnic minorities or LQBTQ status; lack of organization; and systematic degradation and exploitation of disenfranchised or powerless workers.

But, as religious individuals, our posture of kindness, compassion and respect should apply equally to our engagement with the economy, informing our relationship to the human beings at the heart of every financial and industrial system. The Jewish tradition has much wisdom to share on the dignity of work, the fundamental importance of workers' rights and their obligations to their employers, and specific complexities of labor law.[77] This moral argument arising from the sources of Jewish law is complemented and intensified by the religious ethos of Hasidism.

The third point of mutual concern shared by Jews and Catholics involves a vision of fundamental human dignity that extends beyond the need to demonstrate respect and care through economic processes.

---

[76] See http://www.usccb.org/issues-and-action/human-life-and-dignity/economic-justice-economy/upload/catholic-framework-economic-life.pdf, no. 2. Accessed January 8, 2018.

[77] See the wonderful study by Jill Jacobs, *There Shall Be No Needy: Pursuing Social Justice Through Jewish Law and Tradition* (Woodstock: Jewish Lights, 2009); and Ariel Evan Mayse, "The Divine Image: Theological Reflections on Jewish Labor Law," *Kashrut and Jewish Food Ethics*, ed. Shmuly Yanklowitz (Boston: Academic Studies Press, forthcoming).

This world is host to a pervasive atmosphere, the commodifying culture of late capitalism, in which it is common to hear inquiries about the "value" of other humans in monetary terms. Questions such as, "How much is he worth?" should produce shame, for they reveal something quite deep about our collective psyche and the stock we put in material gains rather than spiritual and ethical achievement.

The eighteenth-century Hasidic master Rabbi Nahman of Bratslav was gravely concerned with the way that human beings are easily controlled by their lust for money. Such anxiety lies at the heart of one of his famous tales, which were remarkable in their ability to speak to the imagination and the heart. The story known as the "Tale of the Master of Prayer" includes a striking caricature of a rich but feckless country that has been corrupted by its obsession with money.[78] The land is a place of great wealth—indeed, it is the source of money—but the inhabitants' behavior is bizarre and their mannerisms peculiar. As the tale continues, we learn that these oddities stem from their craven system of values. Anticipating Ayn Rand's utopian vision by over century, Rabbi Nahman's fictional dystopia offers a cautionary tale of a kingdom that measures the worth of an individual by their richness and fortune alone. The wealthiest individual of all, of course, is the king, but he is also the most depraved. This Hasidic tale is a tale of greed run amok to the point of absurdity, but it is a chilling tale that has proven to be an unfortunate portent of modern economic realities.

In contemporary Jewish life, the spiritual energies of Hasidism are unfortunately marshalled in the service of nationalism, of racism, of xenophobia.[79] Understandable in the late eighteenth century, these

---

[78] Arnold J. Band, *Nahman of Bratslav: The Stories* (New York: Paulist Press, 1978), 211-250.

[79] Jonathan Garb, *The Chosen Will Become Herds: Studies in Twentieth-Century Kabbalah*, ed. Yaffah Berkovits-Murciano (New Haven and London: Yale University Press, 2009), 37-51; idem, *Yearnings of the Soul: Psychological Thought in Modern Kabbalah* (Chicago and London: The University of Chicago Press, 2015), 78-103. For a personal reflection, see Don Seeman, "The Anxiety of Ethics and the Presence of God," *A New Hasidism: Branches*, ed. Arthur Green and Ariel Evan Mayse (forthcoming).

teachings cannot be maintained in a world in which our relationships with non-Jews have moved beyond the medieval stigmas held by both parties. There is still anti-Semitic stereotyping in the world, and we condemn it as backward; we surely do not want to be guilty of the same. Notions of Jewish supremacy, which form a direct line from medieval Jewish literature and into Hasidism, are all the more egregious – and dangerous – in a time and place where Jews have returned to power and must once more learn to wield it over others. It is not uncommon. It breaks my heart to aspects of Hasidism sadly mobilized by extremists in an attempt to prove the inhumanity of the contemporary enemies of the Jewish people.

But Hasidism teachings emphasize the infinite power of the human soul, of the capacity – of compassion, of song, and of tears – to unlock even the most tightly-shut gates. Hasidic descriptions of a natural capacity for love, an inborn spiritual faculty for altruism and self-transcendence, should now be extended to all mankind and thus interpreted as an element of the human condition. This innate spiritual faculty in *all* people manifests itself as the heartfelt quest for the Divine, in theologies that call for moral courage, and, more broadly, in our ability to rise beyond the constraints of the ego and reach for the Infinite. It can be fostered through education, stirred through moments of contemplative awareness, and awoken through the honest confrontation with our fellow human beings.

Abraham Joshua Heschel often challenged his students to explain the deeper meaning behind the biblical interdiction against making an image of the Divine. Such renderings are forbidden, said Heschel, not because they are impossible, but because man-made symbols and their natural limitations cannot do justice to God's infinite majesty. "There is something in the world that the Bible does regard as a symbol of God," said Heschel. "It is not a temple or a tree, it is not a statue or a star. *The symbol of God is man*, every man… [who] must be treated with the honor due to a likeness representing the King of kings.[80] The only fitting representation of the blessed Holy One is that of the human being, whose worth and capacity for growth are indeed immeasurable. No molten god or statue can convey the dynamic presence of the human being, and this is what it means to be created in the image of the Divine – to look at the self and all others as infinitely capable of change, or transformation, of ever higher degrees of compassion, love, and open-heartedness

The fourth and final point is the oft-forsaken call to inwardness, to contemplative presence, to the infinite value of the word. In contemporary society, the word has been devalued to the absurd. The mind is cluttered and empty at the same time. Dead words on social media may appear to come to life, flitting across the screen like the fluttering eyelid of a Golden Calf, but the living word has been forgotten. Heschel sought to remind his readers and listeners – Jewish and Christian alike – of the paramount importance of the word. "The renewal of man involves a renewal of language. To the man of our age, nothing is as familiar and trite as words. Of all things they are the cheapest, most abused, and least esteemed… There is no understanding the God of Israel without deep sensitivity to the holiness in words. For what is the Bible? Holiness in words."[81] Heschel understood that Hasidic devotion—and Jewish spirituality—pivots upon the religious power of the word.

Rabbi Dov Baer of Mezritsh, an eighteenth-century Hasidic master of great sophistication and profundity, believed that God's presence is spoken into being precisely through this sacred quality of human language:

> "The heavens were created by the word of Y-H-V-H" (Ps. 33:6), and it is written "and He breathed into him the soul of life [and man became a living soul]" (Gen. 2:7), which is rendered by the Aramaic translation as "a speaking being."[82]
>
> One cannot refer to parts when speaking of God, for He is endless (*ein sof*), and one cannot describe the Infinite as blowing only His

---

[80] Abraham Joshua Heschel, *The Insecurity of Freedom: Essays on Human Existence* (New York: Farrar, Straus & Giroux, 1966), 95. Italics in the original.
[81] Heschel, "The God of Israel and Christian Renewal," 275.
[82] See the translation of Onkelos ad loc.

speech into his nostrils. Therefore, [all of the divine] was included in this speech.[83]

> ... a righteous person's speech is intimately connected (*medubbak u-mekushar*) to its Source. It is just like God's speech, from which heaven and earth were created.[84]

Aristotle defined speech as a uniquely human characteristic, a notion that is reflected in the Aramaic translation of Genesis 2:7.[85] But the Maggid has added what seems to be a highly-original interpretation. The divine word, and the divine essence with it, was breathed into Adam and thus included in the human being for all perpetuity. Rabbi Dov Baer's vision of holy speech reminds me of a repercussive passage from the writings of the incomparable Meister Eckhart, one that I first encountered in my graduate training:

> In the soul's essence there is no activity, for the powers she works emanate from the ground of being. Yet in that ground is the silent "middle": here is nothing but rest and celebration for this birth, this act, that God the Father may speak his word there, for this is by nature receptive to nothing save the divine essence, without mediation. Here God enters the soul with his all, not merely with a part, God enters her the ground of the soul.[86]

God's living vitality, a sacred divine *logos* that fills all words without being constrained by the boundaries of speech, inheres in the heart of *all* human beings. According to this teaching, the Divine sends individuals into this world for the purpose of returning language to its source. In doing so, grafting human speech is grafted back on

---

[83] See Nahmanides' comment to Gen. 2:7. See Moshe Hallamish, "Toward the Source of the Kabbalistic Expression: 'One Who Blows—Blows From Within Himself'," *Bar-Ilan* 13 (1976): 211-223 (Hebrew).

[84] *Likkutim Yekarim*, ed. Avraham Kahn (Jerusalem: 1973) no. 271, fol. 89b.

[85] Cf. Daniel Boyarin, "The Gospel of the Memra: Jewish Binitarianism and the Prologue to John," *Harvard Theological Review* 94, no. 3 (2001): 243-284.

[86] As quoted in Bernard McGinn, *The Essential Writings of Christian Mysticism* (New York: The Modern Library, 2006), 414.

to the Tree of Life, the vital trunk whence all words sprout forth.[87] The redemption of the word is the redemption of humanity, but, moreover, it is the redemption of God from the fractured exile of an imperfect world. This reverence for the word – and for humanity – is one of the great lessons of Hasidism, and it is one that may only be accomplished through open-hearted presence, kindness, and, above, all, through love.

---

[87] On the image of "grafting" as applied to the rejoining of sundered human communities, see *Tsidkat ha-Tsaddik* (Jerusalem: 2002), no. 109; and Romans 11:13-24.

Jewish Historical Testimony at the Table of Christian Hospitality*

JEREMY P. BROWN**

"The guest will judge better of a feast than the cook."

—Aristotle, *Politics*, Book 3, 1282a 20

I. Let Us Now Praise Ill-Mannered Guests

The present volume commemorates the University of San Francisco Speaker Series in the History of Jewish-Christian Relations, an interdisciplinary initiative dedicated to the promotion of an historical-critical ethos for studying and teaching Jewish-Christian relations. In commemorating the series, the volume offers a model for the development of related programing at institutions of higher education, and especially colleges and universities like the University of San Francisco where the development of such programing is circumscribed

---

* Dedicated to Michael Centore, in friendship.
** Jeremy P. Brown is the current Simon and Ethel Flegg Postdoctoral Fellow at McGill University. He taught at the University of San Francisco (USF) in the department of Theology and Religious Studies, and in the Swig Program in Jewish Studies and Social Justice, where he also served as Director of the USF Lecture Series in the History of Jewish-Christian Relations. He earned his PhD in Hebrew and Judaic Studies from New York University.

by an institutional mission articulated in a Christian voice. Within this missional domain, the "guest" speakers prioritized voices of Jewish witness to the historical excesses of Christian hegemony. They brought these voices to light without hedging their testimonies with undue concern for the etiquettes of inter-communal reconciliation. In other words, the speakers personified the fidelity of ill-mannered guests at the table of Christian hospitality. In commemorating the series, I raise some questions about a hospitality complex that binds the differentiated domain of Jewish historical testimony in research and teaching about religion conducted at Christian institutions.

In our collective outcry against the increasingly visible policing of immigration to lands north of the Rio Grande, it has become commonplace, perhaps banal, to appeal to an "Abrahamic" ethical tradition of hospitality. In this generic sense, hospitality can represent a somewhat vague cosmopolitan paradigm that is at once mandated by the scriptural ethics of Judaism, Christianity and Islam. But the framework of hospitality poses many problems. How to foster homecoming that does not exacerbate the proprietary asymmetries that beset host/guest relationships? How to imagine homecoming that is not contingent upon the guest's assimilation of host's values? How to conceptualize homecoming that honors the integrity of host-guest conflict? Writing in an aspirational vein, philosophers and theologians have proclaimed a secularized gospel of radical hospitality, even "impossible" hospitality. In Emmanuel Levinas's phenomenology of hospitality, the host as ethical subject is held "hostage" by an irreducible responsibility to the guest, a dynamic that dislocates the proprietarity typically embodied in hospitable gestures.[1] In the wake of Levinas, Jacques Derrida and Anne Dufourmantelle interrogated the hostilities that come into play whenever conditional *laws* of hospitality limit the idealized "*law* of unlimited hospitality (to give the new arrival all of one's home and oneself, to give him or her one's own, our own, without asking a name, or compensation,

---

[1] Emmanuel Levinas, *Otherwise than Being, or Beyond Essence*, trans. Alphonso Lingis (Pittsburgh: Duquesne University Press, 2006), 79.

of the fulfillment of even the smallest condition)."[2] Somewhat counterintuitively, hospitality can intensify the very hostilities it seeks to overcome. In view of these hospitable hostilities, the imperative to protect bodies and minds targeted by nativist political rhetoric, vigilantism, and the escalation of immigration policing demands also that well-intentioned appeals to hospitality submit themselves to theoretical and historical self-scrutiny.

Such aspirational re-castings of hospitality promoted by contemporary philosophers and theologians play the proprietary asymmetries of host/guest relationships against our expectations, imagining hospitable relationships to be more pliable and reciprocal than inherited models. But even at their most ambitious, host/guest binaries remain an indissoluble feature of the ethical discourse of hospitality.[3] To the extent that religious cultures of hospitality presuppose these binaries, they do not typically incentivize criticism "from below." To the contrary, inflating acts of generosity to sacramental status can have the hostile effect of undermining the criticism of hosts voiced by their guests. When benefaction is sanctified in this way, the beneficiary's criticism becomes blasphemous, or at least, ungrateful or impolite. In what follows, I will apply the criticism of hospitality ethics to a particular field in which a host/guest dynamic obtains. I ask: Does a specifically Christian culture of hospitality reinforce the guest status of Jewish Studies at Christian universities? What are the testimonial conditions foisted upon Jewish Studies as a guest within this domain? What are the epistemological politics that manifest in the name of institutional generosity? Are these rude questions? To whom and why?

I ask these questions as a way of theorizing both the impact and also the limitations of the University of San Francisco Speaker Series on the History of Jewish-Christian Relations. If my intervention strikes defensive readers as ungrateful, impolite, or even blasphemous,

---

[2] Jacques Derrida and Anne Dufourmenantelle, *Of Hospitality* (Stanford, CA: Stanford Univertsity Press, 2000), 77.

[3] Ivana Noble and Tim Noble, "Hospitality as a Key to the Relationship with the Other in Levinas and Derrida," *Theologica* 6, 2 (2016): 47-65.

I hope to provide tools for exploring the deep, historically ingrained structures informing such reactions. Of course, speaking in defense of ill-manners means moving beyond a conciliatory approach to studying the relational history of Judaism and Christianity. But arguments for ditching the conciliatory approach regnant in the disciplines of Theology and Religious Studies are nothing new. My intervention lies in confronting an academic culture of Christian hospitality as an instrument of the conciliatory impulse that undermines the historical testimony that Jewish Studies brings to the proverbial table.

II. Telling and Listening to Unredeemable Stories

The late rabbinics scholar Jacob Neusner denounced the lack of authentic dialogue on the part of both Jewish and Christian scholars. He expressed his frustration from the privileged position of Pope Benedict XVI's (Joseph Ratzinger's) openly polemical Jewish interlocutor. Writing in the *Jerusalem Post* (May 29, 2007) about his ahistorical work of Jewish theology *A Rabbi Talks with Jesus*—a book discussed in Ratzinger's *Jesus of Nazareth, From the Baptism in the Jordan to the Transfiguration*, Neusner glorified his dialogue with the Pope in rather curious terms.[4] He romanticized the exchange as a nostalgic return to medieval Jewish-Christian disputation, and a decisive departure from a politically driven, if intellectually deficient approach to interreligious dialogue.

> In the Middle Ages rabbis were forced to engage with priests in disputations in the presence of kings and cardinals on which is the true religion, Judaism or Christianity. The outcome was predetermined. Christians won; they had the swords. But in the post-WW II era, disputations gave way to the conviction that the two religions say the same thing and the differences between them are dismissed as trivial. Now a new kind of disputation has begun, in which the truth of

---

[4] Jacob Neusner, *A Rabbi Talks with Jesus* (Montreal: McGill-Queen's University Press, 2000); and Pope Benedict XVI, *Jesus of Nazareth, From the Baptism in the Jordan to the Transfiguration* (New York: Doubleday, 2007).

the two religions is subject to debate. That marks a return to the old disputations, with their intense seriousness about religious truth and their willingness to ask tough questions and engage with the answers. [...] For the past two centuries Judeo-Christian dialogue served as the medium of a politics of social conciliation, not religious inquiry into the convictions of the other. [...] In [Ratzinger's book] *Jesus of Nazareth* the Judeo-Christian disputation enters a new age. We are able to meet one another in a forthright exercise of reason and criticism.

I share frustration with the trivializing politics of interreligious conciliation, but Neusner's intervention creates more problems than it solves. When exactly did a conciliatory politics come to dominate interreligious dialogue? Did the problem begin after the second world war, that is, as a post-Holocaust or even post-conciliar (i.e. after *Nostra Aetate*) phenomenon? Or did it begin gradually about two centuries ago, with the advent of religious liberalism? This is unclear. But more pressingly, Neusner's glorification of returning to a pre-conciliatory and plainly belligerent phase in the history of Jewish-Christian relations is both historically and politically farcical. Return to a time when "the Christians had the swords"? This way of romanticizing his exchange with the Pope allowed Neusner to project a heroic image of himself in the guise of the towering leaders of medieval Jewry: Rabbi Yeḥiel ben Joseph at the Paris Disputations of 1240, Naḥmanides at the Barcelona Disputations of 1263, inter alia. These polemicists, we are supposed to believe, embraced the brazen nature of their vocation without mincing words or veiling the extent of their anti-Christian animus. For Neusner, proceeding to a post-conciliatory phase (or even returning to pre-conciliatory phase) involved the removal of all political barriers impeding the practice of authentic interreligious theology, that is, an interreligious theology that does not obfuscate the fact of confessional difference.

Though sympathetic to the foregrounding of Jewish-Christian difference, I am primarily interested in articulating an historical rather than confessional model for the study of Jewish-Christian relations. In other words, I want to promote a model of studying and teaching Jewish-Christian relations that prioritizes historical practice above theological speculation, at least, in a manner that does not require any confessional commitment of its protagonists. Thus, the reader will not mistake my argument for an exercise in dogmatics. At the table of Jewish theological dogmatism, historians of Judaism are likewise summoned to indecorous acts of testimony. And with respect to medieval nostalgia, dispatching with the goal of interreligious conciliation is emphatically *not* equal to the glorification of interreligious violence.[5]

It can be instructive to compare examples of a post-conciliatory approach to the past from the horizon of contemporary politics. Truth and Reconciliation Committees (TRCs)—established at sites of past (and sometimes ongoing) human rights trauma—work to make known histories of political violence, to facilitate healing and forgiveness between victims and perpetrators, and to promote conviviality. A recent book by Abena Ampofoa Asare, bearing the provocative title *Truth Without Reconciliation*, argues in the face political optimism, that TRCs are "complex instruments that consistently evade the expectations of historical revelation and political change embedded in their very name."[6] One problem with a model of truth that is overly burdened by a politics of reconciliation from

---

[5] On the Neusner-Ratzinger relationship, see Aaron Hughes, *Jacob Neusner: An American Iconoclast* (New York: NYU Press, 2016), 248-250. For some earlier approaches to the politics of inter-faith reconciliation, see Arthur Cohen, *The Myth of the Judeo-Christian Tradition* (New York: Harper and Row, 1957); Mark Silk, "Notes on the Judeo-Christian Tradition in America," *American Quarterly* 36 (1984): 66–85; Jacob Neusner, *Jews and Christians: The Myth of a Common Tradition* (London and Philadelphia: SCM Press and Trinity Press International, 1991). For more recent approaches, see Susannah Heschel, "Revolt of the Colonized: Abraham Geiger's *Wissenschaft des Judentums* as a Challenge to Christian Hegemony in the Academy," *New German Critique* 77 (1999): 61–85; the essays collected in Emmanuel Nathan and Anya Topolski, *Judeo-Christian Tradition?: A European Perspective* (Berlin: De Gruyter, 2016); and Healon Gaston, *Imagining Judeo-Christian America: Religion, Secularism, and the Redefinition of Democracy* (Chicago: University of Chicago Press, 2019).

[6] Abena Ampofoa Asare, *Truth Without Reconciliation: A Human Rights History of Ghana* (Philadelphia: University of Pennsylvania Press, 2018), 1.

the outset is that such a model will rarely yield revelations beyond the juridical determination of perpetrator and victim. Important as such a model is for juridical process, "[t]he TRCs romance with the language of victims and perpetrators comes at a cost."[7] It does not serve the subtler purpose of supporting the broadest spectrum of testimony that emerges through a dynamic attunement to victims' narratives. For Asare, the archives produced by Ghana's National Reconciliation Commission (NRC) render audible a dense cacophony, "a conflicted and disorienting clamor of narratives."[8] The scholar suggests that we should embrace a cacophonous construction of truth, one that prompts a fuller democratization of testimony. Accordingly, "when truth is democratized, there is a fundamental shift in the subject and content of political history."[9] This shift yields the insight that "human rights victims are more than objects of pity or rescue, they are experts whose voices illuminate the dilemmas of poverty, inequality, violence, and injustice."[10] Asare's insistence on a more democratized model of testimony, one privileged above the immediate project of social harmony is a fruitfully challenging analogue to a "truth without reconciliation" approach to the history of Jewish-Christian relations. Asare insists that recognizing and valorizing the expertise of those who endure testimonial asymmetries helps to diminish their image as mere "objects of pity or rescue."

Do hospitable overtures to Jewish historical testimony in the arena of Christian academia magnify an image of the guest as an object "of pity or rescue"? To be sure, intra-ecclesiastical calls to repentance for the sins of anti-Jewish violence have a pivotal, even prophetic function. James Carroll is arguably the most outspoken contemporary proponent of intra-ecclesiastical rebuke as a response to Jewish historical testimony.[11] On the stage of interreligious

---

[7] Ibid, 124.
[8] Ibid, 8.
[9] Ibid, 4.
[10] Ibid, 4-5.
[11] James Carroll, *Constantine's Sword: The Church and the Jews — A History* (Boston: Houghton Mifflin, 2001).

conciliation, scenes of rebuke may even facilitate "the healing of memory."[12] But there are serious risks at stake when the academic discipline of Jewish Studies yokes itself to performing the "guest labor" of Christian conscience. As important as historical rapprochement is to the basic integrity of Christian life, when the chief, or even sole function imagined for Jewish witness is to expedite such work in the academic arena, the situation for Jewish Studies becomes one in which its autonomy is sacrificed for the expiation of Christian souls. Such an instrumentalization of the field inflames the very memory that reconciliation seeks to heal, especially when this happens on the institutional stage of Christian universities.

Beyond expiation, the conversation about intercommunal reconciliation often avails itself of figures and images from the theological imagination of redemption. Let us be clear that, historically speaking, both Judaism and Christianity have, *mutatis mutandis*, imagined endtime scenarios of redemption vindicating the one true religion and vanquishing its confessional opponent. Such conceptions of history which presuppose an eschatological resolution are structurally incompatible with the embrace of testimonial cacophony promulgated by Asare. Even within popular post-secular consciousness, vestiges of religious eschatology still inform the entitled assumption that justice prevails, and history more-or-less works out in the end. But in the twenty-first century, who remains in the charmed position to blithely affirm that everything really happens for a reason? Does this somnambulant view of the past not favor the experiences of those whose privileged trajectories are not set too far off course by a few apparently incidental hard knocks? Such a post-secular teleology, closer to the Hollywood ending than Kingdom Come, poses major obstacles to opening one's ears to the clamor of conflicting narratives about interreligious polemic and violence. In other words, just as it is necessary to redraw the parameters of academic programing on the

---

[12] Paul Ricoeur, "Can Forgiveness Heal?," in *The Foundation and Application of Moral Philosophy: Ricoeur's Ethical Order*, edited by Hendrik Opdebeeck (Leuven: Peeters, 2000), 31-36.

history of Jewish-Christian relations to curb the conciliatory impulse, it is all the more so critical to suspend the expectation of a redemptive resolution to interreligious history. Although the example of the Holocaust is both an extreme and hackneyed test-case for thought experiments, it certainly gives the lie to redemptive conceptions of history in which justice prevails with finality.[13] Other episodes from the long history of Jewish-Christian relations would suffice to disrupt the redemptive telos, as would an inestimable number of examples from outside of the boundaries of Jewish history. Looking back on the work of the USF speaker series, I remember it as a forum for telling and listening to unredeemable stories, stories told by souls courageous enough to hold their ground in the face of the crushing social pressure to either consign the past to oblivion, or—which sometimes amounts to the same—to redeem past injuries by means of obliviating mechanisms of reconciliation set upon the table of Christian hospitality.

Lest the reader misconstrue my ill-manners for anti-Christian polemic, I will elaborate on this last point. As much as the Second Vatican Council represents a monumental watershed in the history of interreligious relations, one which explicitly repudiates antisemitism, it is often overlooked that 1965's *Nostra Aetate*, a "Declaration of the relation of the Church to Non-Christian Religions," fails to endorse a conception of interreligious rapprochement that is based upon either a lucid investigation of the past or even its popular recollection. In fact, it does just the opposite. When invoking the history of interreligious conflict between Christians and Muslims, the declaration makes the following recommendation.

---

[13] See for example Zachary Braiterman, *(God) After Auschwitz: Tradition and Change in Post-Holocaust Jewish Thought* (Princeton, NJ: Princeton University Press, 1998); on the Holocaust as impetus for interreligious conciliation, see Massimo Giuliani, "The Shoah as a Shadow upon and a Stimulus to Jewish-Christian Dialogue," in *The Catholic Church and the Jewish People: Recent Reflections from Rome*, edited by Philip Cunningham, Norbert Hofmann, and Joseph Sievers (New York: Fordham University Press, 2007), 54-72.

> Since in the course of centuries not a few quarrels and hostilities have arisen between Christians and Moslems, *this sacred synod urges all to forget the past and to work sincerely for mutual understanding* and to preserve as well as to promote together for the benefit of all mankind social justice and moral welfare, as well as peace and freedom.[14]

I have already discussed various ways in which pairing truth with reconciliation may result in distorting the past. Here, in the very document celebrated as the way forward from interreligious conflict, we are confronted with a model of interreligious understanding that explicitly endorses, even "urges" historical oblivion. The outmoded idea that reconciliation goes hand-in-hand with forgetting—one disseminated by a religious institution with a poor track record where the perpetration of violence is concerned—is perhaps the most urgent justification for my firmness on the need for truth without reconciliation in the forum of academic research on religion. I cannot bring to bear the historical and theological scholarship on Vatican II and religious pluralism upon this very general discussion. However, I also single out the issue for the personal and institutionally-particular reason that as a representative of the Department of Theology and Religious Studies at USF, I am expected to endorse a pedagogy of "religious diversity" that is "encouraged by Vatican II's stance on the Catholic Church's relationship with other faiths" (see D-2 Theology learning outcomes).

III. Why We Need a Genealogy of Sacramental Hospitality

How does the long and varied history of religious hospitality inform the current cosmopolitan discourse of social ethics? Since they either claim to draw inspiration from the generic matrix of "Judeo-Christian" or "Abrahamic" tradition, or explicitly mandate social ethics as the requirement of denominationally specific pre-commitments, it is incumbent upon those who enjoin their communities to hospitality

---

[14] *Nostra Aetate*, §. 3; my emphasis.

in the name of religion to shed light on this question. The imperative is arguably more urgent for those who preach hospitality in academic communities, where resources for doing historical research on religion are ready at hand. In this context, I cannot review the history of religious hospitality with any kind of scope or finesse. But I will distill a few examples that reveal the deep structures within the sacramental discourse of religious hospitality that privilege the proprietary domain of the host in ways potentially hostile to the differential testimonial priorities of guests.

Consider the sacramental scene in which a host receives her guest as Christ. Since antiquity, Christians have taken up the Patristic injunction of preparing a chamber in one's home—a "Christ Room"—to receive the stranger as the very personification of Christ.[15] To be certain, this sacramental framework has potentiated a staggering number of truly praiseworthy Catholic social projects. In fact, the heroic leadership of Peter Maurin and Dorothy Day exalted this sacramental approach to hospitality.[16] My goal is not to cast aspersions on a time-honored and deeply impactful discourse of social ethics. Leaving that positive appraisal *firmly* in place, it must nonetheless become obvious to its proponents that sacramental hospitality is not a framework founded upon values of religious pluralism. Moving as it is to divinize the stranger at the door, sacramental frameworks of divinization constellate doctrinally specific theologies and start from the presumption of confessional sameness. This presumption can be welcoming or alienating depending in large part upon the character and degree of the stranger's strangeness. Is the guest-as-Christ reception a welcome model for non-Christian wayfarers? For stranger strangers? It can effectively reduce non-Christian difference to the status of mere appearance. When receiving the Jewish or Muslim guest as Christ, the host may avow a certain docetism with respect to the guest's non-

---

[15] John Chrysostom, *Homilies on the Acts of the Apostles and the Epistle to the Romans* (Grand Rapids, MI: Eerdmans Publishing, 1997), Homily 45, on Acts 20:32, 277.

[16] Dorothy Day, *House of Hospitality* (New York: Sheed and Ward, 1939), xxvi.

Christianity. In the case of Jewish wayfarers, the practice imposes a Christological narrative onto the guests' apparent vulnerability, without appreciating that Jewish vulnerability is constituted by traumas sustained—either directly, inter-generationally, or even culturally—by violence perpetrated by Christians, at times, in the name of Christ.

On the other hand, if we look at the ideal of monastic hospitality countenanced by the Rule of Saint Benedict, one that served as a model for so much medieval regulatory literature, we find a politics of stratification to be inseparable from the guest-as-Christ reception. This is evident from the outset of Chapter 53, "On the reception of guests (*De hospitibus suscipiendis*)," which begins: "Let all guests who arrive be received as Christ, because He will say: 'I was a stranger and you took Me in' (Mt 25:35). And let due honor be shown to all, especially (*maxime*) to those 'of the household of the faith (*domesticis fidei*)' (Gal. 6:10) and to wayfarers."[17] Though the Rule stipulates that monks receive all guests with honor, humility, care, and kindness, those of "the household of faith" are apportioned special honor. The language of domestic fidelity betrays the judgment that visiting monks and clerics reside, by virtue of both their confession and their vocation, within a proprietary domain that does not extend to all Christians, much to less non-Christians. This is an obstacle to projecting a Levinasian ethics of alterity onto monastic social ethics. The Rule continues: "As soon as a guest is announced, then let the Superior or one of the monks meet him with all charity, and first let them pray together, and then be united in peace. For the sign of peace should not be given until after the prayers have been said, in order to protect from the deceptions of the devil." Christ comes knocking, but the monk cannot be certain He is not the devil, not until the guest demonstrates his bona fides by praying with the host in the name of Christ. In other words, the stranger's divinity remains ambivalent until his confessional strangeness is dispelled.

---

[17] Julie Kerr, *Monastic Hospitality: The Benedictines in England, c. 1070- c. 1250* (Woodbridge, UK: Boydell Press, 2007), 94-120.

If non-Christians risked subjecting themselves to such suspicion, relinquishing or dissimulating testimonial difference was a condition of access. To what degree did medieval monastic hospitality really extend to strangers? To confessional strangers? If this model is not suitable for Christian universities in the twenty-first century, let the administrators disambiguate appropriately by historicizing institutional values.

I have mentioned various ways in which bracketing the project of inter-communal reconciliation potentiates the scholarly vocation of Jewish Studies. Another way it does this is by creating a platform for Jewish Studies to testify in an historically critical way concerning the traditional limitations of rabbinic hospitality as a platform for pluralism. Though like the Benedictine model, rabbinic models of hospitality are typically focused on receiving the intra-communal guest, they do not routinely espouse a sacramental rationale.[18] A piece of rabbinic wisdom attributed to the third-century Babylonian sage Abba Arikha (or simply "Rav") holds that "Welcoming guests is *greater* than greeting the Shekhinah (the divine presence)."[19] This aphorism, which became a popular Mussar aphorism, disentwines the ethical imperative of hospitality from the sacramental motivation of receiving the divine presence, leveraging the inter-personal over the human-divine axis. However, a paradigmatic example from medieval Judaism typifies a less discriminating orientation that I do not hesitate to classify as sacramental. I am referring to a Kabbalistic model for receiving guests into one's Sukkah during the Feast of Tabernacles (see figure below for an image of a family dwelling in a Sukkah from a medieval Italian prayerbook).[20]

According to a famous discussion in the Zohar that provides the textual basis for subsequent iterations of the rite, one welcomes the Ushpizin (Aramaic for guests) who arrive on successive nights

---

[18] On classical rabbinic hospitality, see Christine Hezser, *Jewish Travel in Antiquity* (Tübingen: Mohr Siebeck, 2011), 89-119.
[19] Babylonian Talmud, *Shabbat* 127a.
[20] *Forli Siddur*, 1383, Moses ben Jekutiel Hefetz of the Tzifroni family, ms British Museum Add. 26968.

of the festival as the very Patriarchs Abraham, Isaac, Jacob, Joseph, Moses, Aaron, and David, respectively.[21] The Patriarchal guests personify different attributes of the Godhead. Their arrival announces the gradual homecoming of divinity to the Sukkah, attribute-by-attribute throughout the weeklong celebration.[22] Whosoever fails to accommodate his impoverished guests to the fullest extent brings divine judgment upon himself. To the best of my knowledge, scholars of the Zohar have not before compared the divine Ushpizin to the guest-as-Christ model of hospitality. Despite their incommensurable frames of religious reference, the two models are not dissimilar in reifying doctrinal domains of hospitality that limit receptivity to testimonial difference.

---

[21] Zohar III: 103b-104a.
[22] See Joel Hecker, *Mystical Bodies, Mystical Meals: Eating and Embodiment in Medieval Kabbalah* (Detroit: Wayne State University Press: 2005), 177-8.

שמן עצרת חסור · וסוכה בשמיני
ספק שבועי · מיהב יהבינן מבֿ כרכי
לא מברכינן   מברכינן

נמצא עכשו חג הסוכות

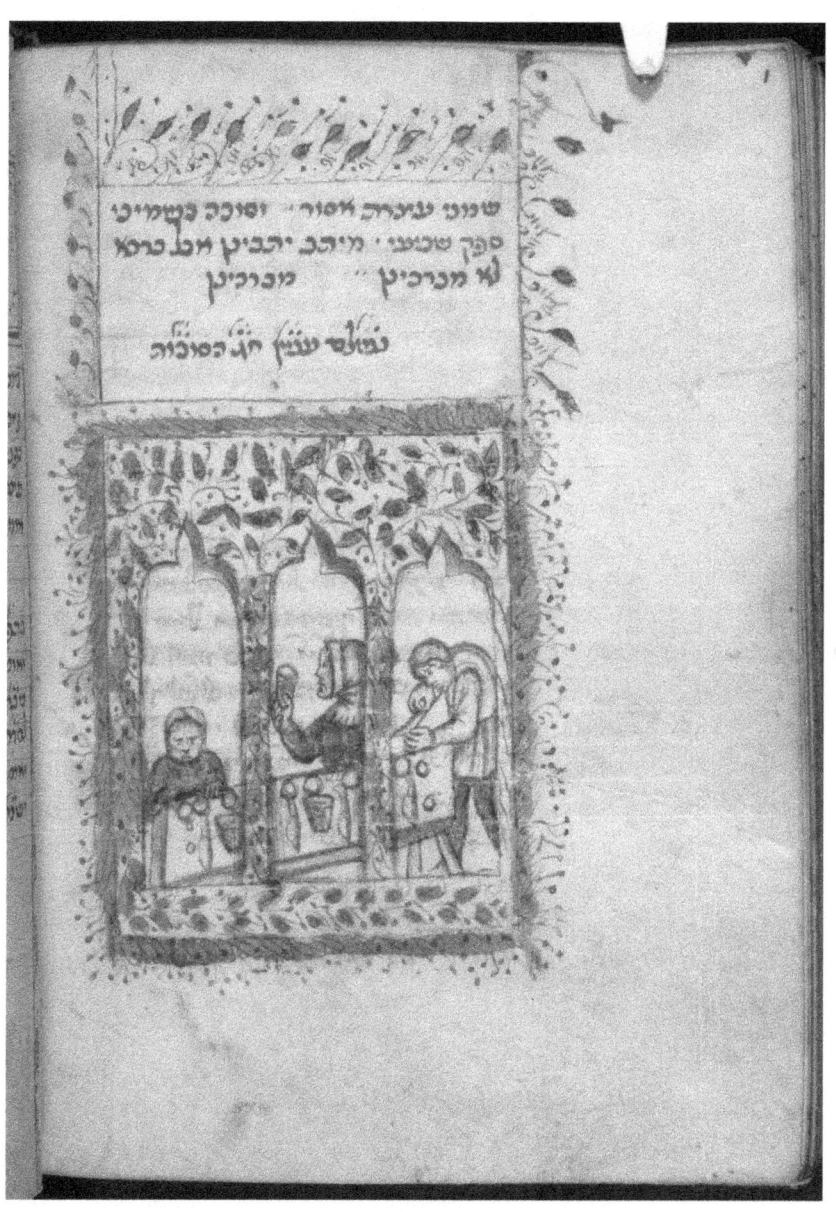

IV. Upholding Historical Priorities

Staying with the theme of liturgical calendars, I turn to the synchronous celebrations of Passover and Holy Week, when interreligious conflict between Jews and Christians reaches its highest pitch. Some of this tension can be attributed to the ritualized antagonism of Jews by Christians as alleged persecutors of Jesus in the days leading up to Easter. In its own rite, the Passover liturgy is full of polemical anti-Christian symbolism.[23] But given the audacious public face of Christian anti-Judaism, and its disproportionate tendency to breach the threshold separating polemical rhetoric from physical violence, I focus here on the enmity of Christians against Jews.[24] Such enmity was especially apparent during the commemoration of Good Friday, when many Christians since the middle ages dramatized Christ's sufferings in high profile public spectacles, through the staging of passion plays. In these plays, actors perform the conflict between Jesus and the Pharisees described in the canonical Gospels, the latter cast as diabolical conspirators against the innocent Nazarene.

Throughout the long and varied history of passion play productions, from medieval Germany to the present-day Philippines, the figure of Judas Iscariot represents the prototypical embodiment of Jewish evil. In particular, the cathartic depiction of Judas' suicide-by-hanging (based on Matthew 27:1-10) has captivated generations of devoted spectators. The horrific image of a Jew hanging from a tree functions as a potent symbol for the insufferable burden of Jewish guilt.[25] The image also illustrates the ostensibly just vindication of Jesus'

---

[23] See Israel Yuval, *Two Nations in Your Womb: Perceptions of Jews and Christians in Late Antiquity and the Middle Ages*. Trans. by Barbara Harshav and Jonathan Chipman (Berkeley: University of California Press. 2006), 56-91.

[24] For a bold history of xenophobic violence in Judaism, see Elliott Horowitz, *Reckless Rites: Purim and the Legacy of Jewish Violence* (Princeton, NJ: Princeton University Press, 2006).

[25] See figure immediately below, from the Psalter-Hours of Guiluys de Boisleux, France, Arras, after 1246; Morgan Library, New York, ms M.730 fol. 14b.

perfect innocence. In vivid detail, the scripts of medieval German passion plays contain stage directions indicating how this scene should be performed. One contains a description of how the young priest playing the role should conceal within his costume a leather sack containing both pig entrains and a live black squirrel. When suspended from the gallows, the script directs Judas to burst open the sack. The actor ejects the intestines from his torso, and liberates the black squirrel—representing the traitor's demonic soul—to scamper off into the netherworld. In other instances, the actor loosed a black raven, producing a similar effect.[26]

---

[26] Annette Weber, "The Hanged Judas of Freiburg Cathedral: Sources and Interpretations," in *Imagining the Self, Imagining the Other: Visual Representations and Jewish-Christian Dynamics in the Middle Ages and Early Modern Period*, edited by Eva Frojmovic (Leiden: Brill, 2002), 165-188, here 182.

Eventually, actors playing this role realized that they were up against some very treacherous occupational hazards. In 1437, during a production in Metz, a young priest playing the part of Judas nearly died when suspended at the gallows. Fast forward to 2012, tragedy struck a twenty-seven-year-old man named Tiago Klimeck while playing the role of Judas in a Good Friday passion play performed in Itararé, Brazil. Sources reported that, during the hanging, four full minutes passed before spectators, thinking the limp body part of the act, recognized that something had gone terribly wrong. A harness malfunction caused the actor to sustain severe brain traumas. Heartbreakingly, the actor perished two weeks later as a result of his injuries. In view of the dangers of having actors stage the hanging, many productions have opted, instead, to hang an effigy of Judas.

In spring of 2016, amid the intense outrage against the Republican US presidential candidate's anti-immigrant and Hispanophobic slander, Mexico City literally ignited in a religious demonstration of resistance. Papier-maché Judas effigies, which for generations have hung and burned in public displays throughout the city, now appeared in the candidate's image. During Holy Week in 2017, 2018, and 2019, other Mexican cities also incinerated effigies of the now president in the rites of the *Santa Quema de Judas*. I point to this particular issue because it demonstrates, in a very tangible way, how an important motif in the history of Jewish-Christian relations continues to acquire ever new horizons of meaning. Here, the narrative of Jesus' persecution by the Jews, and by Judas in particular, serves as a template for investing contemporary struggles against tyranny with religious significance. In the *Quema de Judas* performances, such struggles are reflected in the mirror of medieval, and even ancient Christian anti-Judaism. The dramatic practice of burning Judas-as-Trump effigies during Holy Week is, in fact, a creative and powerful way for Mexican Catholics to imagine their political empowerment on the global scene. But, for all their redemptive promise, these performances mobilize old Christian anti-Jewish values in the pursuit of geopolitical emancipation. To sharpen the contradiction, the rite effectively rehearses xenophobic stereotypes in the very struggle against xenophobia. Such contradictions become discernable precisely by upholding the critical historical priorities I have emphasized throughout.

V. Historical Talking Points for Teaching Jewish-Christian Relations

While teaching at USF, I presented the speaker series in conjunction with an undergraduate survey course called "The Jewish Christian-Relationship." The course, which I designed with valuable input from both Robert Chazan and Clare B. Fischer, constituted a two-millennium journey condensed into the itinerary of single semester. In it, students learned to read primary documents as witnesses to the long interreligious relationship between Jews and Christians. These documents included Biblical texts, Patristic heresiology, Rabbinic literature, examples of Jewish and Christian liturgy, codes of Canon Law, texts of medieval disputations, Jewish accounts of the Crusades and Spanish expulsion, the writings of Luther, treatises on toleration by John Locke and Thomas Jefferson, examples of racial antisemitism in modern Catholic newspapers, Nazi Protestant theology, *Nostra Aetate*, transcriptions of Jewish-Christian dialogue in Latin America, and interviews with Pope Francis. At this point, I will discuss just a few of the talking points that were mainstays of the course, which embraced the same historically critical ethos of the speaker series.

a. Out from Abraham's Tent

There is perhaps no image of hospitality more iconic than the Genesis 18 episode of Abraham and Sarah hosting three angelic visitors at the Terebinths of Mamre. (See below for iconic image of the three angels as the Holy Trinity, i.e. a specifically trinitarian model of sacramental hospitality.[27]) There has been no figure more commonplace to the conciliatory phase of interreligious research than Abraham. Now scholars are reappraising the cost of using the language of "Abrahamic Religions" as a shorthand for the scriptural faiths of Judaism, Christianity, and Islam. In her ground-breaking book, *The Family of Abraham*, Carol Bakhos documents the interreligious fissures concealed within the categorical tent of Abraham.[28] Based on a painstaking analysis of the representation of Abraham and his family in classical biblical and Qur'anic exegesis, Bakhos writes, "an

---

[27] Andrei Rublev "Троица," 1425, Trinity Lavra of St. Sergiua Monastery, Sergiyev Posad, Russia.
[28] Carol Bakhos, *The Family of Abraham: Jewish, Christian, and Muslim Interpretations* (Cambridge, Mass: Harvard University Press, 2014).

emphasis on the common spiritual threads, the shared scriptural heritage and ethical teachings, can lead to major differences being swept under the rug and, ironically, breed misunderstanding."[29] I have adopted Bakhos' paradigm in my teaching by encouraging students to recognize how, when understood in historical context, traditional accounts of the patriarch and his family in Judaism, Christianity, and Islam have been deployed to produce polemical cleavages between competing religious communities. Thus, one talking point, which typically engenders a lively conversation among students is whether these considerations render the very terminology of "Abrahamic religions" obsolete.[30]

---

[29] Ibid, 1.
[30] See too Aaron Hughes, *Abrahamic Religions: On the Uses and Abuses of History* (New York: Oxford University Press, 2012); and Jon D. Levenson, *Inheriting Abraham: The Legacy of the Patriarch in Judaism, Christianity, and Islam* (Princeton: Princeton University Press, 2012).

b. Fraternal Fictions and Frictions

Along the same lines, the rhetoric of fraternity often invoked in the discourse of interreligious conciliation poses similar problems. Though affirmed by academic theologians outside the realm of magisterial teaching,[31] we can look to the current Pope for a recent and prominent deployment of this rhetorical figure. On January 17, 2016, Francis addressed the Great Synagogue of Rome (*Tempio Maggiore di Roma*) with a statement about Jewish-Christian brotherhood. He was explicit in modeling this gesture after John-Paul II's much lauded visit to the synagogue on April 13, 1986, the first Papal visit to the synagogue since antiquity.

> In interreligious dialogue it is fundamental that we encounter each other as brothers and sisters before our Creator and that we praise him; and that we respect and appreciate each other, and try to cooperate. And in the Jewish-Christian dialogue there is a unique and particular bond, by virtue of the Jewish roots of Christianity: Jews and Christians must therefore consider themselves brothers, united in the same God and by a rich common spiritual patrimony, on which to build and to continue building the future. With this visit I am following in the footsteps of my Predecessors. Pope John Paul II came here 30 years ago, on 13 April 1986; and Pope Benedict XVI was among you six years ago. John Paul II, on that occasion, coined the beautiful expression "elder brothers", and indeed you are our elder brothers and sisters in the faith. We all belong to a single family, the family of God, who accompanies us and protects us as his people. ("Visit to the Synagogue of Rome, Address of his Holiness Pope Francis")

The historical irritant that is obscured by the Pope's apparently gracious gesture is that John-Paul II did not coin the phrase "elder brothers" to represent the family relationship of the Church to the Jews.

To the oblivious ear, the positioning of the Church as the younger sibling sounds like an expression of humility. But in the historical

---

[31] See John Connelly, *From Enemy to Brother* (Cambridge, MA: Harvard University Press, 2012).

arena of theological competition between Jews and Christians, no objective has been more polemical than that of securing the blessed portion of the younger brother. Indeed, the typological representation of Church and Israel in the fraternal roles of Jacob and Esau goes back to the writings of Paul, which cast the Church as Rebecca's second born. Writing in an apostolic voice, Paul claimed (Romans 9:12) that the ancient prophecy concerning these enemy brothers, "the elder shall serve the younger" (Genesis 25:23), referred to the servitude of Israel (i.e. "Carnal" Israel) by the Jesus movement (i.e. the "True" Israel). Conversely, Jewish texts have traditionally maintained their ancestral identification with Jacob-Israel. Moreover, they have typically inverted the terms of Paul's exegesis to identify Esau with Rome and the Church. Understood in rabbinic terms, the prophesied servitude of Esau to Jacob refers to the eventual overturning of Christian hegemony and vindication of Israel at the time of the redemption. I hesitate to accuse the Pope of nefarious motives in deploying the rhetoric of fraternity (and that of elder-younger sibling relationships in particular) in his conciliatory mission. Whatever his intention, the fraternal rhetoric not only chafes against the agenda of historical understanding, but risks recapitulating the old polemic. The same criticism may be applied to another polemical motif in the history of Christian representations of biblical brothers. I am thinking of Augustine's interpretation of the Cain-Abel relationship. This is another sibling pair where the older brother is the bad guy. For Augustine, the fratricidal figure of Cain who murders his innocent brother corresponds to the deicidal image of the Jews who ostensibly killed their blameless younger brother Jesus.[32] This case should suffice to illustrate the ease with which even well-intentioned invocations of interreligious fraternity can drift into a polemical register that both distorts the past and incites conflict. Counter-intuitively, one may observe a host of rhetorical features common to both conciliatory and polemical discourses that facilitate an elision of the iron-clad difference supposedly demarcating the two.

---

[32] Paula Fredriksen, *Augustine and the Jews: A Christian Defense of Jews and Judaism* (New Haven: Yale University Press, 2010), 264-270.

And this is to say nothing of the patently androcentric paradigm promulgated by both the patriarchal rubrics of "Abrahamism," and the representation of interreligious relationships in fraternal images.

c. Christianity from Judaism, or Judaism from Christianity?

Another lively talking point related to both the polemical and conciliatory identifications of the Church as younger brother is a kind of "chicken or the egg?" debate concerning the historical emergence and differentiation of Judaism and Christianity. As Pope Francis' address exemplifies, Christians traditionally embrace a narrative of Jewish origins. Whether in affirming an historical fact, avowing a supersessionist paradigm, or both, contemporary Christian theologians rarely question the anteriority of Judaism. Until quite recently, Jewish historians have been on board with this basic trend. Now, in response to the provocations of Berkeley-based scholar Daniel Boyarin, researchers have begun to rethink the conceptual underpinnings of this apparently uncontroversial idea.[33]

Which religion came first, Judaism or Christianity? Prima facie, nothing strikes students as inherently troubling in posing such a straightforward question. But doubts come into play when students ascertain that the very terms they need to ask this question—"religion," "Judaism," and "Christianity"—had not yet been coined (at least, according to their modern acceptations) at the time when most presume the relational individuation of Judaism and Christianity occurred, during the first two centuries of the common era. According to Boyarin, these terms do not obtain what we might think of as a "religious" significance until roughly the mid-third century. At that point, the terminology is defined as a function of the Patristic campaign to "invent" Christianity as a domain of orthodoxy, as a coherent set of beliefs and practices "separated from the locativity of ethnic or geocultural self-definition" ascribed to Christianity's

---

[33] Daniel Boyarin, *Judaism: The Genealogy of a Modern Notion* (New Brunswick, NJ: Rutgers University Press, 2019).

anti-type, namely, Judaism.³⁴ In other words, the term "Judaism" (*Ioudaismos*) first proliferates less as a kind of "religious" self-designation for Judeans than as an antagonistic construction deployed by early Christian heresiographers. In this sense, the "corporate body of Orthodox Christianity, "[t]he *Ekklesia* [...] invents 'Judaism' as an alternate, as the dark double of the true *Ekklesia*, transforming Jews from a People to an *Ekklesia* via the medium of orthodoxy, an *Ekklesia* that it names *Ioudaismos* in Greek."³⁵ As constituted by the discourse of the Church fathers, "*Christanismos* and *Ioudaismos* are two *doxas*, two theological positions, a wrong one, and a right one, a wrong interpretation of the legacy of the prophets, and a right one." Boyarin charts a semantic shift in the terminological acceptation of "Judaism," from a category of ethnic belonging to a way of designating a non-Christian constellation of piety and belief. In this sense, Christianity, in administering its regime of orthodoxy, created Judaism in its own negative image while projecting its own self-image against the relief of its Jewish shadow. The problem of when and how Jews begin to identify positively with "Judaism"—in the sense of a "religion"—is really a belated issue, one, which according to Boyarin, reveals more about the modern exigencies of Jewish participation in Christian society than it does the ancient world.

My criticism of Boyarin is that he weakens the basic datum of Jesus's Jewishness. Of course, scholars have carefully documented and analyzed the work of racist theologians who disputed that datum.³⁶ If Judaism was not created until the Church Fathers expressed it from the "entrails" of orthodoxy in the third and fourth centuries, then the negative premise of Aryan Christology was, in a sense, correct. In other words, by Boyarin's argument, Jesus was not Jewish, at least,

---

34 See Rowan Williams, "Does it Make Sense to Speak of Pre-Nicene Orthodoxy?," in *The Making of Orthodoxy: Essays in Honour of Henry Chadwick*, edited by Rowan Williams (Cambridge: Cambridge University Press, 1989), 3; cited in Boyrain, *Judaism*, 107.
35 *Judaism*, 107.
36 Susannah Heschel, *The Aryan Jesus: Christian Theologians and the Bible in Nazi Germany* (Princeton, NJ: Princeton University Press, 2008).

if "Jewish" means something substantive in relation to "Judaism" as a "religion." Even though Boyarin maintains that some kind of proto-Judaism (a pre-"ism"-Judaism) gave rise to Christianity in the first place, that would only make Jesus a proto-Jew. What are the implications of playing so loosely with Jesus's Judaism? While several critics have appropriately questioned the strong philological angle taken by Boyarin, and I have my own reservations, I nonetheless find his "troubling of the waters" effective in stimulating course discussions about the anachronisms and prejudices sedimented into some of the most intuitive language we use to talk about religious difference.

VI. Conclusion: Leveraging a Broader Conversation

While I doubt that all of my colleagues will embrace the argument adumbrated here, I cannot but speculate that such a plea issuing from Islamic Studies would meet with even less approbation. On April 10-11, 2015, my colleague Aysha Hidayatullah convened a national conference called "Islam at U.S. Jesuit Colleges and Universities," in which leading experts discussed the implications of coordinating Islamic Studies with the Ignatian mission of Jesuit learning. At the conference, various participants extolled the virtues of hospitality. This may be an appropriate way to embark on the many productive conversations stimulated by the landmark conference. But to the degree that the tacit guest status of Islamic Studies at Christian institutions is basically analogous to the situation of Jewish Studies (and to speak of analogy is not to deny key differences), the framework of hospitality will not yield an equitable platform for research and teaching. If readers are persuaded by the truth-potentiating promise of removing the conciliatory expectations placed on researchers of non-Christian religions and cultures by their Christian host institutions, the question of who is advancing the argument may be inconsequential. When considered from a purely structural perspective, one abstracted from the particular interests of either Jewish or Islamic Studies, the demand for reconciliation between hospitably coordinated parties places disproportionate constraints on the testimony of the guest. While I have framed my discussion to address the situation of Jewish Studies at institutions beholden to a Christian mission, there remains the related question of how the apparitions of this hospitality-reconciliation-complex manifest themselves in secular (or secularizing) universities, that is, at institutions still permeated by vestiges of Christian academic culture. Are Jewish Studies and Islamic Studies, to use the examples at hand, mere guests on the academic scene? To what extant is research into non-Christian religions and cultures within the analogously "hospitable" arena of the post-confessional university likewise beholden to regimes of truth which overtly encourage, but tacitly impede?

www.ingramcontent.com/pod-product-compliance
Lightning Source LLC
Chambersburg PA
CBHW022001100426
42738CB00042B/1150